Olive Green: Learning English through a Mystery Drama (CEFR-B1)

CEFR B1

ASARI Yoko
KANNO Satoru
KUBO Takeo
SATO Ryosuke
SIMPSON William

Asahi Press

音声再生アプリ「リスニング・トレーナー」を使った音声ダウンロード

朝日出版社開発のアプリ、「リスニング・トレーナー（リストレ）」を使えば、教科書の音声をスマホ、タブレットに簡単にダウンロードできます。どうぞご活用ください。

◉ アプリ【リスニング・トレーナー】の使い方

《アプリのダウンロード》

App Store または Google Play から「リスニング・トレーナー」のアプリ（無料）をダウンロード

App Storeはこちら▶

Google Playはこちら▶

《アプリの使い方》

① アプリを開き「コンテンツを追加」をタップ
② 画面上部に【15699】を入力しDoneをタップ

音声・映像ストリーミング配信 》》》

この教科書の音声及び、付属の映像は、右記ウェブサイトにて無料で配信しています。

https://text.asahipress.com/free/english/

はじめに

　本書は、映画Olive Greenを題材とし、学習者のリスニング能力とスピーキング能力のさらなる向上を目的として作成されました。この映画は英語学習用に特別に撮り下ろされ、CEFRに準拠しつつ文法事項が導入されています。この映画を繰り返し視聴することにより、学習者は過度な負担を感じることなく、リスニング能力のレベルアップを行うことが可能となります。

　本書はCEFRのB1レベルに対応し、A1レベル、A2レベルに対応する前2冊の続きとなる3冊目として出版されました。ストーリーも1冊目、2冊目の続きとなります。このため、必要に応じ、受講生と一緒に1冊目、2冊目に対応する動画をご視聴ください。

　また、各シーンの会話部分のみを録音し直している音源もあり、明瞭な音声で聴きたい場合やディクテーションの際に活用することができます。

　本書の特徴として、各Unitのスピーキング練習用のアクティビティが挙げられます。スピーキング・アクティビティは、そのUnitで導入された文法項目の学習を意図しています。ペア・ワーク、グループ・ワークを通し、学習者はスピーキング能力を向上させることができます。

　リスニングとスピーキングの2つの能力は、日本人学習者にとって苦手とされてきましたが、実際の言語使用においては必要不可欠です。また、近年では、多くの英語検定試験でこの2つの能力を測るテストが導入されています。本書を通し、技能向上の一助となることを願っております。

執筆者一同

■各Unitの構成

本書のUnitは主に次のものから成り立っています。

The target of this unit is to understand:

学習する文法事項が最初に示されています。どのような文法事項を学習するのか、初めに確認しておきましょう。

Review Activity

1つ前のUnitで導入された文法事項を復習するためのアクティビティです。主に、ペア・ワークを使ったスピーキング・アクティビティとなっています。

Warm-Up

学習する映画のシーンを見る前に、Warm-Upとして、どの部分に注目すればよいかが導入されています。英語で2つの質問が書かれていますので、映像を見る前に質問に答えてみましょう。

Let's Watch!

映画のシーンを理解するのに必要となる単語・句・文が掲載されています。あらかじめ発音・意味などを確認しておきましょう。また、この部分には、スクリプトの一部が空欄で提示されています。ディクテーション用のアクティビティとしても活用できます。

> 注：一部のシーンで英語の非母語話者が登場します。発話が標準英語から逸脱している場合であれ、スクリプトには発話通りの英語を掲載しています。

Comprehension Check

さまざまな内容確認用の問題を通し、それぞれのシーンの内容を確認することができます。

Grammar

それぞれのUnitで焦点が当てられている文法事項を確認してください。学習する文法事項はCEFR におおむね準拠しています。

Speaking Activity

スピーキング用のアクティビティが掲載されています。ペア・ワークやグループ・ワークを通し、 スピーキングの練習をしていきましょう。

Role Play

Unitの内容と関連する3人程度の人物の会話が載っています。発展的な内容となっており、シーン では含めることができなかった単語・表現を練習する機会となります。

Contents

■Main Characters

David Owen: a police officer

Gennady: Sergey's father

Olive Green: an art thief
She stole important business data
from Robert Murray.

Sergey: Gennady's son

Vlad: a hitman

Olive Green

Learning English
through a Mystery Drama

CEFR-B1

Asahi Press

At the Russian Mafia's Office

The target of this unit is to understand:

· Present perfect continuous vs. present perfect

· Typical time expressions: *for* and *since*

Talk with your partners.

1. Have you ever borrowed money from someone? Who and why?

2. In the future, would you like to have children?
   What kind of person would you like them to be?

Scene 1-1

Words and Phrases

 CD: Track **02**

gamble: My brother gambled in cards and lost a lot of money.

heavily: I borrowed heavily from a bank.

at least: You have to be in bed for at least another night.

half a year: Ken lived in the US for half a year.

mostly: There were mostly girls in the classroom.

dog fight: Dog fights are not allowed in this country.

miss: She never misses the morning weather forecast.

I beg you!: Let me go! I beg you!

Script of the Scene

CD: Track **03, 04** / DVD: **Chapter 01** (00:01-00:58)

Gennady: 159,000. ... Listen, your boy has [1]( ) gambling heavily [2]( ) at least half a year or so ... [3]( ) dogs ... What do you mean "dogs"? ... Dogs. ... No, I'm not talking about dog races. [4]( ) [5]( ). Your son has not [6]( ) a single dog fighting event in over two months.

Woman: Give me some time. I [7]( ) you.

Words and Phrases

CD: Track 05

major: My professor had a major influence in my life.

disappointment: He never shows any disappointment to his son.

witness: She witnessed a car accident on her way to work.

graduation: Graduation ceremonies are held in June in the US.

waste of time: Going to the gym is a waste of time for me.

beginner: I'm a beginner of chess.

team up with: The teacher teamed Yuki up with Joe.

loyal: The singer has many loyal fans.

organisation (organization): WHO is an organisation to protect our health.

get in touch with: Can you get in touch with Mrs. Suzuki?

beloved: Sarah is my beloved wife.

Script of the Scene

CD: Track 06, 07 / DVD: Chapter 02 (00:59-02:45)

Gennady: All right. You know, I have a son, too, and much like your son, he's also a [8](   ) disappointment. You have got [9](   ) [10](   ), yes?

Yuri: By the way, boss, isn't Sergey coming home today?

Gennady: Tomorrow. He wants me to go to Oxford to [11](   ) his graduation. [12](   ) of [13](   ) if you ask me. But I have got a plan. I have a job for him. An easy one. Perfect for a [14](   ). And I'm going to [15](   ) him [16](   ) with Vlad.

Yuri: But ... Vlad's a... shit. He's a...

Gennady: A real man. A fighter. A [17](   ) member of this ... organisation. And that is who I want my son to become. So, tomorrow when ... Oh bollocks.

Sergey: Why the hell didn't you come to my [18](   )? I've been trying to [19](   ) in [20](   ) with you all morning.

Gennady: Sergey, my [21](   ) son.

Comprehension Check

Exercise 1 Who are they? What is their relationship?

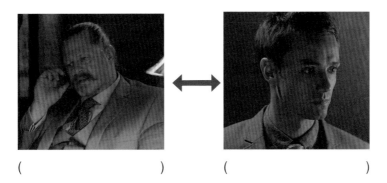

(   )   (   )

Exercise 2 True (T) or false (F)?

1. (   ) Gennady was talking to the woman about his dog.
2. (   ) Gennady accepted the woman's request.
3. (   ) Gennady wants his son to be a real fighter.
4. (   ) Sergey has been trying to talk to Gennady all day.
5. (   ) Sergey graduated from Cambridge.

Exercise 3 Answer the following questions.

1. Why is the woman in trouble?
   (   )
2. How much time has he given the woman?
   (   )
3. What does Gennady want his son and Vlad to do?
   (   )
4. Why is Sergey angry at his father?
   (   )

Exercise 4 Discuss the following topics with your partners.

1. What do you think about gambling?
2. Would you like your family members to attend your graduation ceremony?

Grammar

Present perfect continuous vs. present perfect

Present perfect continuous

→ **To talk about past actions that have recently stopped**

Has it been raining? The grass is wet.
Sorry, I'm home late. I've been studying in the library.

→ **To talk about past actions that are still continuing**

Turn the TV off now! You've been watching TV for four hours!
How long have you been studying English?

Present perfect

→ **To talk about a state that has been continuing for a while**

My brother has lived in New York for five years.
Mr. and Mrs. Sasaki have been married for 20 years.

→ **To talk about experiences up to the present**

I've met the Prime Minister.
Haruki Murakami has written many novels in his career.

→ **To talk about actions that happened in the past and are important in the present**

Oh no! I've lost my key and can't get in.
Oh no! I can't graduate. I've failed the math test.

∗ Notes

State verbs do not usually take continuous forms.

O I have known him for 2 years .
✕ I have been knowing him for 2 years.
O She has always believed in my words.
✕ She has always been believing in my words.
O He has liked the idea of taking part in this project.
✕ He has been liking the idea of taking part in this project.

Typical time expressions: *for* and *since*

for

→ **Used to express how long something has continued**

I've been waiting for you for half an hour. The movie has already started!
She has been reading *War and Peace* for 20 weeks. It's so long!

since

→ **Used to express when something began**

This restaurant has been here since 1988.
Mindy has been living in India since she was ten years old.

Exercise 1 Fill in the blanks by changing the forms of the verbs in ( ) with either present perfect or present perfect continuous.

1. Catherine is one of my friends. I (   ) her for more than ten years. (know)

2. I can't go to school tomorrow. I (   ) my leg. (break)

3. He (   ) his car key for many hours now and it seems he hasn't found it yet. (look for)

4. My father (   ) to New York already, but I didn't say goodbye to him. (fly)

Exercise 2 Fill in the blanks with either *for* or *since*.

1. They got married in 1990 and have been together (   ) more than 30 years now.

2. (   ) Minjun was a high school student, his parents have been running a Korean restaurant.

3. He's a workaholic. He hasn't gotten much sleep (   ) days now.

4. They've been good friends (   ) childhood.

Exercise 3 Correct a mistake in the underlined part of the sentence.

1. It has snowed heavily since midnight and it still doesn't seem to stop.

(   )

2. I read books all the time. I've been liking reading books since I was young.

(   )

3. I've been hating the smell of natto since I first tasted it long ago.

(   )

4. The computer has made a strange sound all morning. I think I need to take it to a repair shop.

(   )

TASK: Decide who should receive the **Most Inspirational Person Award.**

Step 1: Read about the following people.

Emma Watson

Occupation: Actress, an advocate for UN Women's HeForShe campaign

Achievements: Graduated from Brown University, won many awards including Young Artist Award and Teen Choice Awards

Influence: Promoting gender equality

Cristiano Ronaldo

Occupation: Soccer player

Achievements: Received five Ballon d'Or/ FIFA Ballon d'Or awards, won over 300 trophies and medals (by 2021)

Influence: Made many donations including donating £5 million to help the aid effort in Nepal following the earthquake and donating more than $165,000 to fund a cancer center in Portugal

Michelle Obama

Occupation: Attorney and author

Achievements: Former first lady of the United States (2009-2017), wrote a memoir "Becoming" which sold over 10 million copies, started many campaigns such as Let's Move Campaign and Let Girls Learn Initiative

Influence: Inspiring young people to enroll in higher education, tackling childhood obesity in America

Step 2: In your group, decide who should receive the **Most Inspirational Person Award.**

Listen and fill in the blanks.

Jimin: I think ₁ _____ should win the Most Inspiration Person

Award because she has won many awards.

Daiki: Yes, ₂ _____. But ₃ _____ has won

many awards, too.

Bruno: Well, ₄ _____, I think education is very important, so

₅ _____ Michelle Obama should be the winner.

Daiki: Yeah, ₆ _____. I didn't know much about her. I

just knew her as the former first lady of the US. But it looks like she

₇ _____ to help young people.

Jimin: I still think ₈ _____ deserves to win. She is so talented and

she ₉ _____ gender equality. I looked into the HeforShe

Campaign and it's really interesting.

Bruno: This is such a hard task. Okay. Let's do a little bit of research about these people.

Once we ₁₀ _____, let's talk together again.

9

Unit
2

Gennady and Sergey

The target of this unit is to understand:

· First conditional
· *Unless*

Review Activity

Work in pairs. Ask your partners the following questions.

· Name one thing you have been doing for more than five years.
· Name three accomplishments that you are proud of.

Warm-Up

Talk with your partners.

1. What kind of profession would you like to have in the future?
2. Have you ever been asked to do something that you did not want to do?

Words and Phrases

CD: Track 09

probably: He'll probably call you back soon.

knock: The angry neighbor is knocking at my door.

profession: She decided to change her profession.

tuition fee: University tuition fees are too high in America.

fancy: We are going to a fancy restaurant for our date tonight.

screw up: I screwed up! I crashed my mom's car!

be proud to ...: We're very proud to announce our new product.

biologist: Biologists study the life of plants and animals.

hydrologist: Hydrologists study the earth's water.

gift: My brother sent me a nice gift for my birthday.

be supposed to: Take an umbrella with you. It's supposed to rain this afternoon.

whoever: You cannot always go out with whoever you like.

wish: I wish you the best of luck.

keep ... within reasonable bounds: Can you please keep the volume within reasonable bounds?

education: I received an education in the UK.

nightmare: Studying for the entrance exam is a nightmare.

job proposal: My uncle gave me a nice job proposal.

employee: All of the employees are paid well in this company.

Don't even ...: Don't even think about eating my chocolates.

delicate: Politics is a delicate topic at a dinner party.

get involved (in) : Don't get involved in any gambling.

lousy: I got lousy grades last semester.

bright: My dog is bright and knows many tricks.

Script of the Scene

Gennady: You've ¹(   ) still got my old number. You know ²(   ) ³(   ) I need to change these things? If I use the same one for longer than two weeks, the police ⁴(   ) come ⁵(   ) at my door.

Sergey: The police will stop bothering you when you get a normal ⁶(   ).

Gennady: My profession paid your ⁷(   ) ⁸(   ) at bloody Oxford and got you the ⁹(   ) car you came in here. So don't you tell me ... Son, I'm sorry. I screwed up, okay? I'm happy and ¹⁰(   ) ¹¹(   ) have a biologist in the family.

Sergey: Hydrologist.

Gennady: Yes, yes, yes. Hydrologist. Sit down ... I have a ¹²(   ) for you.

Sergey: What am I ¹³(   ) ¹⁴(   ) ¹⁵(   ) with it?

Gennady: ¹⁶(   ).

Sergey: Shoot who?

Gennady: Whoever you wish. But keep it ¹⁷(   ) reasonable ¹⁸(   ), okay? I'm so happy this education ¹⁹(   ) is over. In fact, I have a job proposal for you. I want you to help Vlad, our new ²⁰(   ) from Russia, find someone ...

Sergey: Dad, please, ²¹(   ) ²²(   ) start.

Gennady: No, listen, it is not what you think. It is a ²³(   ) business matter. The police should not get ²⁴(   ). And Vlad is new here. His English is lousy. He does not know the city. Also, he is not ²⁵(   ) enough for this kind of job.

Sergey: Dad, I can't.

<hr>

Scene 2-2

Words and Phrases   CD: Track 12

unless: Unless it rains, let's have a picnic this weekend.

earn: He earned a lot of money from investments.

Just this once: I'll never do it again, all right? Just this once.

brutal: Miki can get brutal when competing.

worry (about): My mom worries about me all the time.

 **Script of the Scene**

Gennady: Son, ²⁶(   ) you do it, I will ask you to get a normal profession and start paying back the money ²⁷(   ) been ²⁸(   ) you for years. That would be what? A few hundred thousand quid at least. How much does a hydrologist ²⁹(   ) these days, huh?

Sergey: Okay, dad, ³⁰(   ) this ³¹(   ). But I'm not doing anything ... ³²(   ).

Gennady: Don't ³³(   ) ³⁴(   ) that.

Comprehension Check

Exercise 1 **What do you think Gennedy's profession is?**

(   )

Exercise 2 **True (T) or false (F)?**

1. (   ) Gennady has a normal job.
2. (   ) Sergey became a biologist.
3. (   ) Sergey is happy to receive a gift from his father.
4. (   ) Gennady helped Sergey financially to study at Oxford.
5. (   ) Sergey finally accepted the job offer from his father.

Exercise 3 Answer the following questions.

1. Why couldn't Sergey get in touch with his father?
    ( )
2. Why does Gennady have to change his phone often?
    ( )
3. What did Gennady give to his son?
    ( )
4. What kind of person is Vlad?
    ( )
5. Why did Sergey accept the job?
    ( )

Exercise 4 Discuss the following topics with your partners.

1. What would you do if your parent(s) had a dangerous job?
2. Do you think university tuition in Japan is expensive?

Grammar

First conditional

If / When + present simple, ... *will*...

... *will* ..., *if / when* + present simple

➜ *If*: possible action / event in the future / we **think** something may happen

I will prepare some delicious food if you come tonight. (I don't know if you are coming.)
If Vlad finds Olive, he will hurt her. (There is a chance that Vlad will not find Olive.)

➜ *When*: we **know** something will happen

I will prepare some delicious food when you come. (I know you are coming today.)
When Vlad finds Olive, he will hurt her. (Vlad will find Olive. It's just a matter of time.)

Unless

➜ *unless = if ... not*

Sergey will not use this gun unless he needs to do so.
   = Sergey will not use this gun if he does not need to do so.

Unless Olive gives the documents back to Gennady, she will have to live in fear.
   = If Olive does not give the documents back to Gennady, she will have to live in fear.

Unless I get a scholarship, I will not be able to go to university.
   = If I don't get a scholarship, I will not be able to go to university.

You're not allowed to enter the building unless you have a permit.
   = If you do not have a permit, you're not allowed to enter the building.

Exercise 1 Write first conditional sentences with *if*-clauses, using the given information.

Condition: you / wash the dishes.　　Result: I / cook dinner tonight.

→ *I will cook dinner tonight if you wash the dishes.*
　Or *If you wash the dishes, I will cook dinner tonight.*

1. Condition: you / not do your homework　　Result: your parents / get angry

   (　　　　　　　　　　　　　　　　　　　　　　　　　　　　　　　).

2. Condition: my sister / have enough time tomorrow　　Result: we / play video games

   (　　　　　　　　　　　　　　　　　　　　　　　　　　　　　　　).

3. Condition: you / study much harder　　Result: you / not regret it in ten years

   (　　　　　　　　　　　　　　　　　　　　　　　　　　　　　　　).

4. Condition: the weather / be fine this weekend　　Result: I / go fishing in the lake

   (　　　　　　　　　　　　　　　　　　　　　　　　　　　　　　　).

Exercise 2 Fill in the blanks with either *if* or *unless*.

1. I won't pay the money (　　　　　　　) you don't send the goods to me next week.
2. I won't go to the party (　　　　　　　) you go. It won't be fun.
3. (　　　　　　　) it rains heavily, I think I'll go for a jog tomorrow morning.
4. (　　　　　　　) you don't help me, I don't think I will be able to finish writing this report.

Exercise 3 Fill in the blanks with either *when* or *if*.

1. (　　　　　) you arrive at the airport, I will pick you up. (You know the person will arrive there.)
2. (　　　　　) you don't know where to go for the summer, maybe he will give you some good advice. (You are still not sure whether the person has fixed the summer plan or not.)
3. Can you bring the book you borrowed from me (　　　　　) you visit our house next time. (You expect the person to visit you again because you want the book back.)
4. (　　　　　) you and your husband would like to go on a trip during this summer, I will take care of your children for a while. (You are not sure whether the person and her husband might go on a trip.)

Exercise 4 Rewrite the sentences by using the words in the parentheses.

1. If you don't wake up at five tomorrow, you will not be able to catch the first train.

   (unless)

   (　　　　　　　　　　　　　　　　　　　　　　　　　　　　　　　).

2. I will not attend Dante's birthday party unless you go. (if)

   (　　　　　　　　　　　　　　　　　　　　　　　　　　　　　　　).

TASK: First conditional game

With your partner, decide who will be A and who will be B. Person A must look at his or her pictures and make a sentence using *If* or *When* within 10 seconds. If he or she cannot make a sentence in 10 seconds, they will not get any points. Whoever gets the most points wins!

Person A

1.

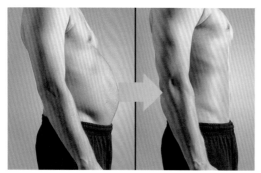

2.

3.

4.

Person B

1.

2.

3.

4.

Role Play

CD: Track 15

Listen and fill in the blanks.

Jimin: Daiki, do you want to go first?

Daiki: No no, 1 _____ .

Jimin: Okay fine. Don't forget to

2 _____ .

Daiki: Oh I won't. Whenever 3 _____ .

Jimin: Ready. So the first one... My mother always prepares snacks for me if

4 _____ .

Daiki: Good sentence and you've got 5 _____ . That's one point. Next.

Jimin: Okay... hmmm...

Daiki: 6 _____ . You have five seconds.

Jimin: Oh no!

Daiki: I'm sorry. 7 _____ . I can't give you a point.

Jimin: My mind went 8 _____ !

On a Mission with Vlad

The target of this unit is to understand:

· *Should*
· *Be allowed to ...*
· *Let / make* someone do ...

Review Activity

Look at the situations below. What will you do if or when you are in these situations?

the weather is bad

graduate

miss a train

hungry

Warm-Up

Talk with your partners.

1. Do you have a driver's license? Have you ever received a traffic ticket?
2. What do you do when you need to kill time?

Scene 3-1

Words and Phrases

CD: Track 16

remove: Please remove the cups from the table.

elbow: He hurt his elbow yesterday.

lever: To stop this machine, you have to pull this lever.

make ... clear: The European countries made their positions clear.

button: The play button is broken.

draw one's attention: The teacher drew the students' attention to climate crisis.

blend in: Melissa blends in well with her colleagues.

aim for: I'm aiming for straight As this year.

Script of the Scene

CD: Track **17, 18** / DVD: Chapter **05** (05:58-07:44)

Sergey: Vlad, [1](   ) [2](   ) remove your elbow from the [3](   )? I'll go and have a look. You stay in the car, okay? And [4](   ) me [5](   ) this clear. You are not [6](   ) [7](   ) touch any buttons. [8](   ), just sit and don't do anything. No, Vlad. You [9](   ) [10](   ) stay in the car. We don't want to draw anyone's attention. [11](   ) [12](   ). This is what we're [13](   ) [14](   ). Okay? What? What do you want?

Vlad: Your gun. Take it. A small man [15](   ) have a [16](   ).

 Words and Phrases

CD: Track 19

vehicle: We must reduce pollution from vehicles.

awfully: It's awfully hot today.

seem to: She doesn't seem to be feeling all right.

Script of the Scene

CD: Track 20, 21 / DVD: Chapter 06 (07:45-08:34)

Police Officer: Sir, please remove your [17]( ). You're [18]( ) [19]( ) [20]( ) park there.

Vlad: Not my car.

Police Officer: But I saw you sitting in it and talking to the [21]( ). Please call him and [22]( ) him [23]( ) it. Now. ... Sir, please stop right now.

Police Officer: You [24]( ) me no choice.

Sergey: I'm [25]( ) sorry, sir. What [26]( ) [27]( ) be the problem?

Comprehension Check

Exercise 1 Who is this man?

(   )

Exercise 2 True (T) or false (F)?

1. (   ) Sergey got out of the car to get some snacks.
2. (   ) Sergey told Vlad to listen to the radio after he left the car.
3. (   ) Sergey doesn't want to attract people's attention.
4. (   ) The police officer saw Vlad talking to the driver.

Exercise 3 Answer the following questions.

1. Why didn't Sergey want Vlad to come with him?

   (   )

2. What did Vlad say Sergey should take?

   (   )

3. What did the police officer order Vlad to move?

   (   )

4. Why did the police officer think that Vlad knows the driver of the car?

   (   )

Exercise 4 Discuss the following topics with your partners.

1. Where would you like to go if you had an expensive car?
2. When do police officers stop to question people?

Grammar

Should

→ **Making a suggestion**

You have a temperature. You should get some rest.

My father has high blood pressure. He shouldn't eat salty foods.

We should go home. It's getting late.

→ **Asking for advice**

I have a test tomorrow. What should I do?

What should we do if there is an earthquake?

Should we take a box of chocolates or a bouquet of flowers to the home party?

* Notes

should = ought to

· *Ought to* is sometimes used to replace *should* but is used less frequently.

· Questions beginning with *ought* are rare.

Be allowed to ...

→ *be allowed to* = to have permission to do something

You are not allowed to take photos here.

We are not allowed to smoke in our dorm but we are allowed to have parties.

Am I allowed to eat this cake? – No, you aren't. It's your sister's.

Let/make someone do ...

→ *let* = to give someone permission to do something

Let me see it.

Our boss lets us use the Internet at work but within reasonable bounds.

Why don't you let us do the work for you?

→ *make* = to force (or cause) someone to do something

His beautiful song made me cry.

My parents don't make me do house chores on week days.

Can you please make your brother stop making that noise!

Exercise 1 Complete the sentences by using *let* or *make* in the right form. Use the words in the parentheses.

e.g., *She was late for the party because you* <u>*didn't let her know*</u> *the time. (her/know)*

1. Can you _____ your room when you move to the new place?

    (me/see).

2. Tom was late again. The teacher _____ not to be late again.

    (him/promise)

3. I asked the doctor if I could check out of the hospital.
    Luckily, she _____ home.   (me/go)

4. My parents didn't _____ to the party because it's so late at night.

    (my sister/go)

5. In my childhood, my parents didn't _____ vegetables if I didn't want
    to.   (me/eat)

Exercise 2 Reorder the words to make a sentence. The first word is not capitalized.

1. (their pets / raise / people / should) with responsibility.

    (   ) with responsibility.

2. (a secret / I / keep / this / should) or can I tell everybody?

    (   ) or can I tell everybody?

3. (their smartphones / allowed / not / use / to / are / students) in this class.

    (   ) in this class.

4. I have a previous appointment. Please (finish / let / this meeting / me) a bit earlier
    today.

    Please (   ) a bit earlier today.

Exercise 3 Make a suggestion with *should* by looking at the picture.

e.g.   1.   2.

e.g., *She* <u>*should get more sleep*</u>*. She looks really tired these days.*

1. It's going to be really cold tonight, so you _____.

2. We _____ because she looks so hungry.

TASK: Talk about your university regulations.

Step 1

A student studying in a university in London uploaded the following picture and comment on her Instagram, and here is what other people said about regulations at their university.

9:41

funny_student

funny_student OMG! I got in trouble for driving into my campus! Do you have any silly rules at your university? #unfairrules #universitylife

youonlyliveonce That's annoying! My university lets us drive to our campus, but we are not allowed to park overnight.

miki111 I'm a university student in Akita and our university makes us take two foreign languages!

xoxoxo @miki111 I think students should learn multiple languages. That's actually a good regulation.

paulandpaula Our university has completely banned smoking on campus. I think they should make a smoking area and at least allow us to smoke there.

Step 2

With the people in your group, think of five regulations that your university makes their students follow.

1. ....

2. ....

3. ....

4. ....

5. ....

Step 3

Choose a regulation that your group thinks should be changed and explain why to your class.

Role Play

CD: Track 22

Listen and fill in the blanks.

Jimin: Let's think of some regulations at our university.

Daiki: There are so many... But the one I hate is ₁ _____ into the university campus.

Bruno: I hate that rule too! I can understand no parking cars at school, but they ₂ _____ our bikes.

Jimin: I know another rule that I think is silly. We ₃ _____ a book from the library for more than two weeks.

Daiki: Actually, I think that's okay. We ₄ _____ it as soon as possible because there might be other students who want to borrow it...

Jimin: ₅ _____.

Bruno: ₆ _____ not missing classes?

Daiki: ₇ _____ on the reason. I think most professors ₈ _____ a class if you are sick or there is a family emergency. We ₉ _____ classes anyway.

Jimin: Daiki, you are such a goody ₁₀ _____.

At the Clothes Shop

The target of this unit is to understand:

· Second conditional

Review Activity

Work in pairs. Ask your partners the following questions.

· What are some things that you were not allowed to do at school?
· What are some things that your parents made you do?
· What are some things that you should do this weekend?

Warm-Up

Talk with your partners.

1. Do you like to go shopping? Where do you usually go?
2. Which fashion brand do you like or don't like?

Scene 4-1

 **Words and Phrases**　　🔊 **CD: Track 23**

solution: The scientist found a solution for the issue.

 **Script of the Scene**　🔊 **CD: Track 24, 25 / DVD: Chapter 07** (08:35-08:54)

Vlad: I ¹(　　　) ²(　　　　) and talk to them. We talk, we
³(　　　) a ... ⁴(　　　　). I come back. You watch the
⁵(　　　). They come out, you ⁶(　　　　) them.

Scene 4-2

 **Words and Phrases**　　🔊 **CD: Track 26**

puzzle: My teacher's angry attitude puzzled me.

popularity: The popularity of smartphones spread rapidly.

polo shirt: Polo shirts have become popular among businesspeople in Japan these days.

unmanly: Sophia doesn't like Noah's unmanly behavior.

popped collar: I like to wear my uniform with a popped collar.

fashion crime: I think wearing a cowboy hat is a fashion crime.

 **Script of the Scene**　🔊 **CD: Track 27, 28 / DVD: Chapter 08** (08:55-09:29)

Olive: One thing that always ⁷(　　　) me is the popularity of
⁸(　　　) ⁹(　　　　) among men. Why would anyone want
to wear ¹⁰(　　　)? They make you look ... well, ¹¹(　　　)
would be the word. And the ¹²(　　　) ¹³(　　　), dear god.
It's a ¹⁴(　　　) ¹⁵(　　　). Look. You'd look so much better
¹⁶(　　　) you ¹⁷(　　　) a plain T-shirt ... Black, white. Maybe
even ¹⁸(　　　) ... Though red ... ¹⁹(　　　) ²⁰(　　　)
²¹(　　　) see you in it first.

David: Olive, would it be okay if you just ²²(　　　) me ²³(　　　) for a
second?

 Words and Phrases

CD: Track 29

horrible: I burnt this meat, and it tastes horrible.

invention: The invention of smartphones has made our lives more convenient.

 Script of the Scene

CD: Track 30, 31 / DVD: Chapter 09 (09:30-09:53)

Vlad: The polo shirt. A horrible ²⁴(   ). What do you think?
²⁵(   ) ²⁶(   ) look like a Brit in a shirt like this? Would I ...
²⁷(   ) ²⁸(   ) ...Olive?

 Script of the Scene

CD: Track 32, 33 / DVD: Chapter 10 (09:54-10:24)

David: Shit, my hand.

Vlad: We must ²⁹(   ) ³⁰(   ) to the shop. You need to pay
³¹(   ) my polo shirt.

Comprehension Check

Exercise 1 Who is this woman? Who is this man? What is their relationship?

(   ) (   )

Exercise 2 True (T) or false (F)?

1. ( ) Olive doesn't like men in polo shirts.

2. ( ) Sergey needs to buy a polo shirt for Vlad.

3. ( ) Olive thinks that a popped collar is a nice way to wear a polo shirt.

4. ( ) David wants Olive to help him to choose a shirt.

Exercise 3 Answer the following questions.

1. In Olive's opinion, how do polo shirts make men look?

( )

2. What type of shirt does Olive think David should wear?

( )

3. What did Olive do when she realized Vlad had been following her?

( )

4. Why did David throw a shopping bag at Sergey?

( )

5. Why did Vlad say that they need to go back to the shop?

( )

Exercise 4 Discuss the following topics with your partners.

1. Do you prefer a plain T-shirt or a polo shirt?

2. Who do you usually go shopping with?

3. Do you like to get fashion advice from your friends? Why or why not?

Second conditional

If + past simple, ... *would / could / might* ...

... *would / could / might* ... *if* + past simple

→ **imaginative, hypothetical, and unreal situations in the present and future**

If I went on a trip around the world, I would be the happiest person in the world. (I'm not going anywhere at the moment.)

We would have time for our hobbies if we didn't work so hard.

If you could fly like a bird, where would you go?

We might have a pet cat if my sister weren't allergic to animals.

*Notes

When *if* is followed by the verb *be*, you can say *if I were, if he were, if she were* and *if it were*.

If I were a celebrity, I would buy houses in Beverly Hills.

If Einstein were alive, science technology would develop even more.

Exercise 1 Fill in the blanks by using the words in the parentheses.

e.g., If I <u>were</u> the prime minister, I <u>would reduce</u> taxes. (be / reduce)

1. Sorry, I've got a cold now. If I _____ sick, I _____
    your house today.   (not be / visit)

2. If you _____ all your money, how _____
    you _____ what you need to survive?   (lose / get)

3. What _____ you _____ if
    you _____ one wish come true?   (do / can make)

4. If I _____ work so late every night, I _____ you
    more often.   (not have to / see)

Exercise 2 Make a hypothetical sentence.

1. It's snowing heavily outside, so we cannot drive far.

    → If it weren't snowing heavily outside, (   ).

2. It's a secret, so I won't tell you about it.

    → (   ), I would tell you about it.

3. I have lots of homework, so I won't watch television tonight.

    → (   ).

4. We speak English, so we understand his lecture.

    → (   ).

Exercise 3 Correct a mistake in the sentence.

1. If I am going to meet the King of England, I would ask him to have tea with me.

    (   )

2. The world will be a better place if there were no war.

    (   )

Speaking Activity

TASK: Second conditional board game

Make a small group. Take turns rolling a dice and making sentences with *If...* on each island. If a student lands on a cloud, the student must make their own second conditional sentence.

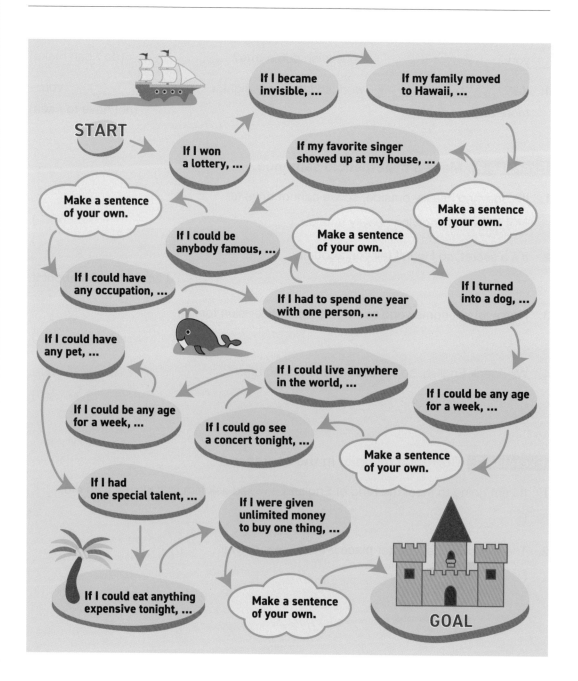

 **Role Play**

CD: Track 34

Listen and fill in the blanks.

Jimin: 1_____ to decide the order?

Daiki: Okay!

Bruno: Yay, I won! Let me start and then we can 2_____.

Jimin: Sure.

Bruno: Okay. I've got a six. It says, "If my favorite singer showed up at my house, ..."

Hmmm... If my favorite singer showed up at my house, 3_____

for me!

Jimin: That's a nice one! Okay. 4_____ now. Two. If I became invisible...

I 5_____ on my brother all day.

Daiki: Hahaha. That's 6_____, Jimin. Do you hate your brother?

Jimin: No, he's cool, but I think 7_____ pretty funny.

Daiki: My turn next. Four. I have to make my own sentence... Let's see... If I

8_____, I 9_____ for children who can't go to

school.

Bruno: That's really nice of you, Daiki. I 10_____ it all on myself.

Truth about Vlad

The target of this unit is to understand:

· *Would = used to*
· *Used to / would* vs. past simple

Review Activity

Take turns asking and answering using second conditional sentences.

e.g., *see the future*

A: If you could see the future, what would you do?   B: I would find out my future partner.

1. go to outer space
2. go back in time
3. become the Prime Minister

Warm-Up

Talk with your partners.

1. Have you ever helped anyone? What did you do for them?
2. Do you owe anyone a favor? Why?

Words and Phrases

CD: Track 35

loose cannon: He is a loose cannon. We can't predict what he will do next.

mindless: He regrets his mindless behavior.

lunatic: I haven't seen such a lunatic.

huge: I was amazed at how huge an elephant really is!

leftovers: My mother made curry and rice using yesterday's leftovers.

posh: I've never been to a posh French restaurant like this.

poverty: This NGO provides education to children living in poverty.

take under one's wing: The aunt took the child under her wing.

debt: Don't shop too much or you'll be in debt.

collect: The sheriff collected information on the man.

run errands: My parents are always so busy that I have to run errands for them.

used to: We used to walk along the river when we were children.

bodyguard: The Secret Service is the presidential bodyguard.

conclude: The party was concluded at 1:00.

transaction: The older generation prefer cash transaction.

trap: We caught a mouse with a trap.

carry: My friends helped me carry the heavy boxes.

blood: Do you have a Band-Aid? I need to stop the blood.

demon: There are many demons in the Greek myth.

owe: I owe the bank a lot of money.

The point is ...: The point is (that) you should be more careful about security.

personal: I can trust my best friend with personal secrets.

tragedy: Shakespeare is famous not only for tragedy but also for comedy.

lately: We haven't had good news lately.

depressed: He is depressed because he failed the exam.

give ... a scare: That car accident gave me a real scare.

 **Script of the Scene**

Sergey: Loose cannon, dad. That's what he is. [1]( ) lunatic. Where the hell did you find him?

Gennady: Listen. I [2]( ) [3]( ) Vlad for 25 years. And you know what? He [4]( ) my life once. We [5]( ) in Russia in [6]( ). It was during Perestroika ... [7]( ) people could get rich quickly. I was like that. Vlad was a boy then. [8]( ) years old. Already a [9]( ) man. But ... he was very poor. He [10]( ) [11]( ) eat the leftovers from bins behind the [12]( ) hotels ... Sergey, you have no idea what [13]( ) can do to your mind. Anyway, I took him [14]( ) my [15]( ) ...

·········

He [16]( ) [17]( ) debts for me, run errands. Also, he [18]( ) [19]( ) [20]( ) as my bodyguard. One day, I was concluding a [21]( ) with a few gentlemen. I [22]( ) they were friends, but it was a [23]( ). One minute we were talking and drinking, and suddenly they all had [24]( ) in their hands. Before I [25]( ), I had one in my [26]( ). And you know what Vlad did? ... Five men. With his [27]( ) hands. Then he [28]( ) me to hospital. They told me later that he [29]( ) [30]( ) through the streets of Moscow all covered in [31]( ) ... like a demon. The [32]( ) is I owe him a lot, yes? And you know ... there [33]( ) [34]( ) some ... personal [35]( ) in his life lately. He came to [36]( ) [37]( ) because he had no choice. He hates [38]( ) here. He's ... well ... [39]( ), I guess. So, I want you to teach him some English, show him things ... help him finish this job. He needs to work. You leave him with nothing to do, he sits in a [40]( ) [41]( ), looking at the wall. It is sad. I want him to be happy [42]( ).

Sergey: Okay, I can be his [43]( ). But promise me this. I am not helping him [44]( ) anyone.

Gennady: No. He will give them a [45]( ), take back what they [46]( ) [47]( ). ... Okay, he may beat them up [48]( ) [49]( ) [50]( ). But I promise you he's not killing anyone.

Sergey: Come Vlad. Let's go and get them.

Comprehension Check

Exercise 1 Which country is this? Which character is from this country?

Exercise 2 True (T) or false (F)?

1. (   ) Gennady and Vlad met in 1998.
2. (   ) Gennady and Vlad were once in Mexico.
3. (   ) Gennady wants Vlad to be happy again.
4. (   ) Sergey agrees to help Vlad murder Olive and David.

Exercise 3 Answer the following questions.

1. In which time in Gennady's life did he become rich?
   (   )
2. Why was Vlad covered in blood?
   (   )
3. What does Gennady want Sergey to do for Vlad?
   (   )
4. What kind of job did Vlad used to do for Gennady in Moscow?
   (   )

Exercise 4 Discuss the following topics with your partners.

1. Have you or anybody you know ever been taken to the hospital? What happened?
2. Which countries in Europe do you want to go and why?

Used to / *would* vs. past simple

→ *used to* / *would*: <u>repeated</u> past actions

> I used to/would run 10 km every morning.
>
> We used to/would have lunch together every Sunday.
>
> She used to/would hold Christmas parties every year.

→ past simple: <u>single</u> past actions

> I met him a few years ago.
> My mom baked a delicious cake yesterday.
> She knocked on the door twice.

✻ **Notes**

We don't usually use the negative or question form of *would* for past habits.

- ○ She didn't use(d) to take a train to work.
- ✕ She wouldn't take a train to work.
- ○ Did you use(d) to go skiing with your family when you were a child?
- ✕ Would you go skiing with your family when you were a child?

We can't usually use *would* to talk about past states.
state verbs: *live* / *like* / *hate* / *know*, etc.

- ○ We used to believe that we could change the world.
- ✕ We would believe that we could change the world.
- ○ They used to love this campsite.
- ✕ They would love this campsite.
- ○ I used to know all the key historical dates from the Middle Ages.
- ✕ I would know all the key historical dates from the Middle Ages.

Exercise 1 Choose the correct form to make a sentence about past habits.

1. My father (used to / would) be a baseball player when he was in high school.

2. (Did Lin and Jacque use to / Would Lin and Jacque) be a couple?

3. We (used to / would) like playing baseball in the park after school.

4. There (used to / would) be a lot of factories in the town where I grew up.

5. My teacher (didn't use to / wouldn't) give us so much homework before.

Exercise 2 Circle the right form. Sometimes two forms are possible.

1. Yesterday, I (went / would go / used to go) camping with my family in Yamanashi.

2. There (were / used to be / would be) so many flowers in this garden 10 years ago.

3. I (met / used to meet / would meet) a beautiful girl on this street many years ago. She looked amazing.

4. I (hated / used to hate / would hate) listening to loud music when I was young.

Exercise 3 Make sentences using *used to / would to* make it true for you.

e.g., *play cards* 1. cook 2. play the piano

3. like bugs 4. get up early

e.g., *I used to / would play cards with friends and I still do.*
　　 I used to / would play cards with friends before, but I don't anymore.
　　 I didn't use to play cards, but I do now.

1. ( ).

2. ( ).

3. ( ).

4. ( ).

Speaking Activity

TASK: Discuss what life was like before smartphones.

Step 1

First, answer the following questions with the people in your group.

1. When did you get your first smartphone?
2. How many hours a day do you spend using your smartphone?
3. What do you use your smartphone for?

Step 2

Think what life was like before smartphones.

	Now	Before
Personal life	✓ Take pictures on the phone	✓ Take pictures with a camera
	✓	✓
	✓	✓
	✓	✓
Work/school life	✓ Keep track of schedule on an app	✓ Use a scheduler
	✓	✓
	✓	✓
	✓	✓

Step 3

Share your ideas with other groups.

e.g., *We take pictures on the phone now, but before smartphones, we used to/would take pictures with a camera.*

Listen and fill in the blanks.

Jimin: I love my phone, and I can't live without it. Life without smartphones must've

been ₁_____.

Daiki: Yeah, it is one of the most ₂_____. So, Bruno, what do you use

your phone for?

Bruno: I use it mainly ₃_____.

Daiki: Me too. I guess people ₄_____ it on their

₅_____ or something like that.

Jimin: That means they ₆_____ it whenever they

₇_____.

Daiki: Yeah, I ₈_____. How sad... I use my phone mainly to

₉_____.

Jimin: I guess people ₁₀_____ to friends before then?

Bruno: Yeah. Or maybe they ₁₁_____ they ₁₂_____

when they saw each other.

Daiki: Actually, that's not such a bad situation. I'm ₁₃_____ texting

friends... It's not really good for my school grades.

Jimin: Maybe life before smartphones ₁₄_____...

Bruno: C'mon, Jimin. You were just saying how you couldn't live without your smartphone!

[Unit 6]

Hotel Hideaway

The target of this unit is to understand:

· *Will*
· *Could / may / might*
· *Can't* and *couldn't, may not* and *might not, won't*

Review Activity

Work in pairs. Ask your partners the following questions.

· What are three things you used to do when you were a child but you don't anymore?
· What are three things you didn't use to do when you were a child but you do now?

Warm-Up

Talk with your partners.

1. When booking a hotel, which one of the following is the most important? The least important? The location, the price, the service?
2. Have you ever had an injury? What happened?

Words and Phrases

 CD: Track 39

hourly: Keisuke works in the convenience store for an hourly wage of 1,000 yen.

rate: The mobile phone company announced a new rate.

affordable: The price of smartphones is not affordable these days.

definitely: Microplastics are definitely harmful to your health.

dislocated: The boxer dislocated her shoulder.

judge: You mustn't judge people by their appearance.

accent: There are many different kinds of English accents.

hitman: The hitman tried to kill the president.

no doubt: Look at the sky. There's no doubt it'll rain.

moment: He fell in love with her the moment he saw her.

over one's head: This is way over my head. Can you explain it more easily?

touching: My brother gave a touching speech at my wedding.

protect: She leads a movement to protect the environment.

disappear: My dog disappeared suddenly.

mess: The prime minister left a mess for his staff to clean up.

leave ... behind ... : I've left all the bad memories behind me.

whole: I presented my idea in front of the whole class.

Script of the Scene

CD: Track 40, 41 / DVD: Chapter 12 (14:35-16:00)

David: Lovely place, Olive. Do you stay here often?

Olive: Every time I'm in London ... They ask zero questions and the [1](   )
[2](   ) is very [3](   ). Now, show me your hand.

David: Ow. They [4](   ) [5](   ) broken. Ow. They are
[6](   ) broken.

Olive: No. Dislocated at most. ... Look, honey, we really [7](   )
[8](   ) talk about our relationship.

David: We do?

Olive: Yes, baby. ... The big guy in the shop ... Judging by the [9](   ), I'd say
he [10](   ) [11](   ) Russian. A hitman, [12](   )
[13](   ) about it. [14](   ) definitely [15](   ) us
the moment he sees us again.

David: Don't you think we should talk to the police? We're in way [16](   ) our
[17](   ).

Olive: David, your trust in the British police is ... [18](   ). But I don't
think they can protect us. Look, we [19](   ) finish this tonight and
[20](   ) together.

David: Disappear together ... Leaving this [21](   ) [22](   ) behind
us. Why [23](   ) we do this my way?

Scene 6-2

🌿 Words and Phrases

🔊 **CD: Track 42**

constable: The constable shot at the thief.

mess up: Paul's mistake messed up the
  plan.

take responsibility for: The president
  refused to take responsibility for the
  military action.

🌿 Script of the Scene

🔊 **CD: Track 43, 44 / DVD: Chapter 13** (16:01-16:13)

Olive: I'm a ²⁴(   ). I don't talk to the police. I ²⁵(   )
      ²⁶(   ) from them.

David: And I'm a police ²⁷(   ). I make sure people who ²⁸(   )
      things ²⁹(   ) take responsibility ³⁰(   ) it.

Comprehension Check

Exercise 1   What are their jobs?

Exercise 2   True (T) or false (F)?

1. (   )   Olive thinks the people in the hotel are nosy.
2. (   )   Olive thinks Vlad is a hitman.
3. (   )   David thinks it's better to get the police involved.
4. (   )   Olive and David talked about their relationship.
5. (   )   Olive thinks David's fingers are broken.

Exercise 3 Answer the following questions.

1. Why did Olive choose this hotel?

   (   )

2. How does Olive know Vlad is from Russia?

   (   )

3. Why doesn't Olive want to report to the police?

   (   )

4. What's wrong with David's hand?

   (   )

Exercise 4 Discuss the following topics with your partners.

1. Have you ever been in a situation that was way over your head?
2. When you cause a problem, do you always take responsibility for it?
3. How many different Japanese accents do you know?

Grammar

Will

→ *will* = assumption based on experience

Don't touch the cat. It will scratch you! It's really afraid of strangers.

Connie will remember the address. Her memory is excellent.

They will be at work now. It's only 2 p.m. and they don't finish until 5.

✽ **Notes**

→ **Degrees of certainty**

· *will definitely = very sure*

The movie will definitely be a hit. It's directed by Spielberg.

Samantha studied for her bar exams for hours and hours everyday. She'll definitely pass!

· *will probably = almost sure*

You should take an umbrella just in case. The weather forecast said it will probably rain today.

Don't worry. Your son will probably be okay. He probably just sprained his ankle.

Could / may / might

→ **Something that is possible to occur/happen**

could / may / might are mostly interchangeable

The weather could/may/might be nice tomorrow.

They could/may/might come late.

We could/may/might get lost without a map.

Can't and *couldn't, may not* and *might not, won't*

→ *can't* and *couldn't* = conviction that something is not true

It can't be Anna. She's not in the country. She's gone to Australia.

You can't be serious! I don't believe you.

She couldn't do it to me. We've got an agreement.

→ *may not* and *might not* = speculation that something is unlikely

They may not come today. I know they worked until late last night.

Sarah might not finish the marathon. She isn't as fit as she was last year.

We might not have time to see everything. Rome is full of great monuments from the past.

→ *won't* = assumption that something is unlikely (based on experience)

They won't lend you any money. They're too stingy.

I can hear someone at the door! It won't be any of your guests. It's too early.

Write the number down for me. I won't remember it otherwise.

Exercise 1 Complete the sentences by choosing expressions from the box.

won't be home / will be busy / could get here / may not be feeling well / might know

1. A: Do you know where the movie theater is?

    B: Sorry. Ask the officer over there. He (   ).

2. A: I don't understand why Emily won't pick up my call!

    B: She (   ).

3. A: I don't know what time Fred is showing up.

    B: He (   ) at any time.

4. A: What time are you coming back?

    B: I (   ) until late tonight.

Exercise 2 Fill in in blanks with either *must* or *can't*.

1. You (   ) be tired after the long travel on the airplane.

2. There was a knock on the door. That (   ) be Cathy. She had left for her school trip last night.

3. That guy often passes by our house. He (   ) live near here.

4. Ken has bought a new car again! If he can afford a Mercedes, he (   ) be short of money.

Exercise 3 Complete the conversation by choosing the right response from (a)-(d).

1. Why can't I call him now?   ———   (a) I'll probably bring my children.
2. What shall we do?   ———   (b) We'll definitely go by taxi.
3. How should we go there?   ———   (c) We could go for a walk.
4. Are you coming to the party alone? ———   (d) He might be sleeping.

TASK: What will happen 30 years from now?

Look at the list. With the students in your group, take turns making questions and making predictions using modals of probability and certainty.

	Student A	Student B	Student C
Robots / do housework e.g., *Do you think robots will do all the housework?*	*might*	*will definitely*	*might*
Cars / run on electricity			
People / fly to space			
Smartphones / no longer be used			
People / no longer shop in stores			
Students / classes online			
Homeless / increase on the streets			
Temperature / continue to rise			
Food / not enough for everyone			
Think of a question			
Think of a question			
Think of a question			

Listen and fill in the blanks.

Jimin: I've never thought about what the world ₁_____ in thirty years.

Daiki: Me ₂_____. Shall we start?

Jimin: Okay. Do you think robots will do all the housework in the future?

Bruno: I don't think they will do all of the housework, but they ₃_____

a lot of it like ₄_____.

Jimin: I agree with you, Bruno. I hope we still ₅_____ our own food. I

just don't think food cooked ₆_____ will be the same as food

cooked ₇_____.

Daiki: How romantic, Jimin. I didn't know you cared so much about

₈_____.

I think all housework ₉_____ by robots.

₁₀_____ us more time to ₁₁_____ other things

like work.

Bruno: Okay. Do you think all cars will run on electricity?

Jimin: Oh I ₁₂_____. If all cars were electric, then we

₁₃_____ about climate crisis.

Daiki: Yeah. But, boy, have we got to do more than electric cars to save this planet from

the crisis!

[Review 1]

1 **Fill in the blanks by changing the forms of the verbs in ( ) with either present perfect or present perfect continuous.**

1. We _____ (know) each other for so many years now.

2. It seems that the rain _____ (stop) now. Children are running outside.

3. Takashi _____ (go) to school already. His bag's not in his room.

4. The guy _____ (run) around the park for many hours now. Is he a professional runner or something?

2 **Correct the mistake(s) in the underlined part and rewrite it.**

1. <u>Have you seen Fiona when you came over here?</u> I've got something to talk to her about.
    (   )

2. <u>Has she ever been playing tennis before?</u> She doesn't seem to know how to hold her racket.
    (   )

3. Since he was young, <u>Ken is showing his talent as a writer to the world.</u>
    (   )

4. <u>Lee has just been completing his homework</u> and now he is ready to watch television.
    (   )

3 **Write first conditional sentences with *if*-clauses, using the given information.**
Condition: you / wash the dishes.   Result: I / cook dinner tonight.
→ *I will cook dinner tonight if you wash the dishes.*
   Or *If you wash the dishes, I will cook dinner tonight.*

1. Condition: our teacher / not give us homework today
    Result: we / go to the baseball game
    (   ).

2. Condition: the weather / not good next week   Result: we / postpone our trip
    (   ).

3. Condition: you / keep talking while he's studying   Result: he / get very angry
    (   ).

4. Condition: you / forget my birthday again   Result: I / never forgive you
    (   ).

4 Fill in the blank with either *if* or *unless*.

1. (   ) you want to publish your books, get a good agent.

2. (   ) we use this machine appropriately, we will get hurt. We need to be careful.

3. He hardly talks much (   ) he is among his close friends. He's not sociable.

4. Please visit our house (   ) you have a chance to come to this town.

5 Complete the sentences by using *let* or *make* in the right form. Use the words in the parentheses.

1. I wanted to go out of the hospital. Unfortunately, the doctor _____ (me / stay) in the hospital.

2. My father _____ (me / drive) his car. The car is one of the most precious things in his life.

3. My boss always _____ (us / work hard) but today he _____ (go / home) early because I had a headache.

6 Reorder the words to make a sentence. The first word is not capitalized.

1. (your car / allowed / are / not / park / to / you) here.

   _____ here.

2. (allowed / am / beer / drink / I / to)?

   _____ ?

3. (go / if / should / we / where) a big typhoon comes near here.

   _____ a big typhoon comes near here.

4. (explain / let / me / reason / that / the) this happened to us.

   _____ this happened to us.

7 Make a suggestion with *should* by looking at the picture.

e.g., *You* <u>*shouldn't eat too much at night*</u>. *You'll gain weight.*

e.g.   1.   2.   3.

1. These days, people are not allowed to smoke in most places, so maybe you _____ smoking.

2. You _____. You don't look well.

3. She _____. She looks really tired these days.

8 Fill in the blanks by using the words in the parentheses.

e.g., *If I* **were** *the prime minister, I* **would reduce** *taxes. (be / reduce)*

1. If I _____ the President of the US., I _____ a peaceful world. (be / make)

2. If we _____ with animals, our lives _____ happier. (can talk / be)

3. If we _____ a creature from outer space, we _____ by them. (meet / attack)

4. If I _____ a chance to meet a singer, I _____ them to sing for me. (have / like)

9 Make a second conditional sentence.

1. We do not study hard, so we cannot follow the class.
   → If we studied hard, ( ).

2. We are not birds, so we cannot fly in the sky.
   → ( ), we could fly in the sky.

3. They are rich, so they do not understand what poverty is.
   → ( ) they would understand what poverty is.

4. The bridge is broken, so we cannot go to the next city.
   → If the bridge weren't broken, ( )

10 Circle the right form. Sometimes both forms are possible.

1. President Reagan (used to / would) be a famous actor and he starred in many movies.

2. There (didn't use to / would not) be many train stations in this town.

3. Which subject (did she / would she) study hard last summer to enter university?

4. We (used to / would) go to USJ when we lived in Osaka.

5. My sister (used to / would) be interested in expensive cars and she had a BMW and a Porsche.

6. My cousin (used to / would) live in Dubai for three years.

11 **Complete the sentences by choosing expressions from the box.**

> can't be / might not be feeling / will probably need / won't move

A: My dog (   ) from the fireplace.

B: He's panting. He must be sick. He (   ) well.

A: That (   ). He was fine just a few minutes ago.

B: He doesn't look fine. You (   ) to take him to a hospital.

12 **Fill in in blanks with either *must* or *can't*.**

1. You (   ) be serious. Your story is totally nonsense.

2. This statue (   ) be made of cheap plaster because it's much cheaper than others.

3. She (   ) be at home. She is always at work this time of day. Let's stop by her house later.

4. He (   ) have a problem because he looks pale and is almost crying.

13 **Complete the conversation by choosing the right response from (a)-(d).**

1. Don't let children touch knives. ___ (a) She will probably be a good doctor.

2. She studies very hard. ___ (b) It won't start up.

3. Something's wrong with this computer. ___ (c) My students may find it boring.

4. This book is for little children. ___ (d) They could get hurt.

[Unit
7]

Sergey Standing Guard

The target of this unit is to understand:

· Past perfect

Review Activity

Work in pairs. Guess the answers to the following questions using *could(n't)/may (not)/might(n't)*.

1.

This is a creature called Nessie.
Guess:

· What kind of creature could it be?

· What might it do?

· Where might you find it?

2.

This is Santa Claus.
Guess:

· How many languages might he be able to speak?

· What might he do during summer?

· How old could he be?

Warm-Up

1. Have you ever made an important promise to anyone? What was it?
2. Have you received any advice? What kind of advice was it?

Words and Phrases

CD (Disc 2) : Track 01

discuss: Let's discuss the problem.

issue: We have a lot of environmental issues.

violence: To stop violence against children, what can we do?

explain: The biologist explained the process of development.

rough up: The gang roughed up the restaurant owner.

a bit: Can you turn up the volume a bit?

That's it.: All you have to do is stand by the door. That's it.

watch one's back: My best friend always watches my back when I get in a fight.

Script of the Scene

CD (Disc 2) : Track 02, 03 / DVD: Chapter 14 (16:14-18:21)

Vlad: You stay here.

Sergey: Remember. ¹( ) ²( ). Just like my father told you.

Vlad: What?

Sergey: What ³( ) you ⁴( ) "what"? When I took this job, I'd ⁵( ) the issue of ⁶( ) with my father. He said he ⁷( ) already ⁸( ) it to you that we're supposed to ... you're supposed to rough them up ⁹( ) ¹⁰( ), take what's stolen and ¹¹( ) ¹²( ). Is that correct?

Vlad: He told you ... that?

Sergey: He made a ¹³( ).

Vlad: Okay, I'll see what I can do. You ... ¹⁴( ) my ¹⁵( ). If something ... happens, use that ¹⁶( ).

......

David: And I'm going to say ... Olive, it's time for you to ¹⁷( ) ¹⁸( ) your ... Oh shit.

Sergey: Oh. ... Not again, please.

Comprehension Check

Exercise 1 Where are Sergey and Vlad?

Exercise 2 True (T) or false (F)?

1. (   ) Vlad was warned beforehand by Sergey's father not to kill.
2. (   ) Vlad advised Sergey to use his knife if necessary.
3. (   ) David senses Olive is in danger.
4. (   ) Olive almost got shot by Sergey.

Exercise 3 Answer the following questions.

1. Why did Vlad tell Sergey to stay in the corridor?
   (   )
2. What did Sergey tell Vlad not to do?
   (   )
3. What must Vlad and Sergey get back?
   (   )
4. What happened to the receptionist?
   (   )

Exercise 4 Discuss the following topics with your partners.

1. What kind of problems have you had recently?
2. What is a better way to solve a problem without using violence?

Past perfect

had (*'d*) + past participle

→ **Used to refers to an activity/event before another action in the past**

I had given up on this project a long time ago.

She'd gone to the office already.

Had he been to Paris before 2020?

Using past perfect and past simple together

Past perfect is used for the earlier of the two past actions/events.

Useful Expressions: *Before, when, already, just, yet*

She had read three books about France before she went to Paris.

The movie had started when we arrived at the cinema.

Had everybody already left when John showed up? Yes, they had.

I came home just as the news had started. I missed the beginning.

It hadn't started raining yet when I left the building.

She had read three books about France before she went to Paris.

NOW

Exercise 1 Circle the right form.

1. Sam (traveled / had traveled) around the world before he (graduated / had graduated) from university.

2. When Charles entered his office, he (noticed / had noticed) something had been moved. Someone (was / had been) in his office.

3. When I got home, nobody was in the living room. Everybody (went / had gone) to bed.

4. When I (got / had gotten) to the cashier, I noticed that I (lost / had lost) my wallet.

Exercise 2 Read the situation and write an appropriate sentence with the words in the parentheses.

e.g., *You met your ex-boyfriend for the first time in 10 years yesterday.*
   → *(I / not / see him for a long time)* <u>*I hadn't seen him for a long time*</u>.

1. I asked if Mike was hungry, but he said he wasn't.
   → (he / just / have / lunch) _____.

2. I wasn't able to see Rachel at the party last night.
   → (she / already / go home) _____.

3. I sat on a seat right next to a guy trembling on the airplane.
   → (he / never / fly / before) _____.

Exercise 3 Complete the sentence by using the past perfect tense.

e.g., *My friend wanted to eat at the new Italian restaurant. I didn't want to because* **(I had already been there many times)**.

1. I wanted to see the new *Spiderman* movie, but my friend didn't want to because
   (_____).

2. I was not scared of traveling to Spain alone because
   (_____).

58

Speaking Activity

TASK: The Best Excuse

Read the following scenario and prepare an excuse. Share your excuse with the people in your group and take a vote for who has the best excuse. You must use the past perfect tense in your excuse (no points are given if you do not use the past perfect tense). The person with the most points wins!

1. I was late for class because...

2. I couldn't clean my room because...

3. I had to break up with my boyfriend/ girlfriend because ...

4. I didn't do my homework because ...

Listen and fill in the blanks.

Jimin: Let's look at the first picture. I was late for class because... Anyone

1 _____ their excuse?

Daiki: Okay, I've got one!

Jimin: Go ahead.

Daiki: I was late for class because I 2 _____ an old lady

3 _____ .

Bruno: Not bad. But is that a 4 _____ excuse?

Daiki: Well then you try, Bruno.

Bruno: Alright. I was late for class because I slept in.

Daiki: That's not good! First of all, you didn't use the past perfect tense. And

also, no teacher 5 _____ to be late for class because you

6 _____ .

Jimin: 7 _____ this then? I was late for class because I

8 _____ on the train and 9 _____ them to the

station staff.

Bruno: Wow! What an imagination! If that 10 _____ , you

11 _____ be excused for being late!

Surprise!

The target of this unit is to understand:

· The order of adjectives
· Adjectives with *-ed* / *-ing*

Review Activity

Work in pairs. Look at the pictures and make sentences using the past perfect tense of the verbs provided in the parentheses.

1. ... before I started tennis

(play Ping-Pong)

2. ... when I arrived at the room

(class / start)

3. I couldn't solve math questions before ...

(enter / junior high school)

4. I wanted to lie down because ...

(eat too much)

Warm-Up

1. Have you ever stopped your friends from fighting?
2. Is there anyone in your family who looks like you?

Scene 8-1

 **Words and Phrases**

 CD (Disc 2) : Track 05

wash: My father washes his car every weekend.

proud: My proud manager would not admit his mistakes.

ox: An ox was used to carry heavy things.

get angry with: The dog got angry with the neighbor's kittens.

be afraid of: The boy is afraid of dogs.

bullet: There was a bullet in the victim's leg.

 Script of the Scene

CD (Disc 2) : Track 06, 07 / DVD: Chapter 15 (18:22-19:42)

Vlad: I thought you should finish [1]( ) your hair. I remember [2]( ) hair was important for my [3]( ), too. She was bigger than you ... [4]( ), [5]( ), [6]( ) woman. Strong as ...er ... an [7]( ). Sometimes ... she got angry with me, I was [8]( ). Fatter here ... much fatter. But her [9]( ) ... like yours.

......

Vlad: I removed the [10]( ) from that one, so no [11]( ), huh? Now you give me the [12]( ), yes?

Scene 8-2

Words and Phrases

CD (Disc 2) : Track 08

psychotic: The news said the psychotic mass murderer was arrested.

unstoppable: The progress of technology is unstoppable.

machine: Are there any vending machines around here?

punch: The boxer punched him on the nose.

fit as a fiddle: Eating vegetables keeps you fit as a fiddle.

Script of the Scene

CD (Disc 2) : Track 09, 10 / DVD: Chapter 16 (19:43-20:22)

David: Go.

Sergey: [13]( ) me [14]( ) to him first. He's a psychotic, unstoppable [15]( ) machine. If you start [16]( ), we're all going to [17]( ).

David: Shut up or I'll [18]( ) you once again.

Vlad: See, Sergey? I've just ... [19]( ) her [20]( ) a bit. But she is [21]( ) as a [22]( ).

Comprehension Check

Exercise 1 **Where is Vlad? What does he want to get from Olive?**

Exercise 2 **True (T) or false (F)?**

1. (　　　) Vlad waited for Olive to finish putting makeup on.
2. (　　　) Vlad had taken out the bullets from the gun.
3. (　　　) Vlad's wife is still alive.
4. (　　　) Olive's eyes remind Vlad of his wife's.
5. (　　　) Vlad was scared of his wife when she was angry.

Exercise 3 **Answer the following questions.**

1. What did Vlad say was important for his wife?
   (　　　　　　　　　　　　　　　　　　　　　　　　　　　　　　　　)

2. What did Vlad compare his wife to when she was angry?
   (　　　　　　　　　　　　　　　　　　　　　　　　　　　　　　　　)

3. What happened when Olive pulled the trigger?
   (　　　　　　　　　　　　　　　　　　　　　　　　　　　　　　　　)

4. How does Sergey describe Vlad?
   (　　　　　　　　　　　　　　　　　　　　　　　　　　　　　　　　)

Exercise 4 **Discuss the following topics with your partners.**

1. What is a daily habit that is important to you?
2. Have you experienced any dangerous situations?

Order of adjectives

A rule to arrange adjectives
○ a nice blue British car   ✕ a British blue nice car
○ a beautiful ancient stone castle   ✕ a stone beautiful ancient castle

1. opinion

nice, fantastic, wonderful, terrible, awful, great, beautiful

2. size

big, small, large, enormous, short, tall, tiny

3. age

new, old, young, ancient

4. shape/style

oval, square, round, rectangular, flat, curly, straight

5. color

red, blue, white, black, yellow, reddish, yellowish, green, golden

6. origin

American, British, European, Roman, eastern, northern

7. material

plastic, leather, paper, wooden, cotton, gold, silk

8. purpose

sleeping (bag), electric (kettle), bath (towel), kitchen (knife)

Adjective endings: *-ed/-ing*

Adjectives formed from verbs (e.g., *annoy, confuse, disappoint, terrify, worry*...)

-ed

→ **Used to describe how people feel**

I was annoyed by their behavior.

She felt confused when she heard the news.

We are disappointed by the result of the meeting.

-ing

→ **Used to describe a thing or situation**

Their behavior was annoying.

The news was confusing.

The result of the meeting was disappointing.

Exercise 1 Put the adjectives in the correct order.

1. a (wooden / nice) desk   → a (   ) desk

2. a (large / blue) sky   → a (   ) sky

3. a (winding / long) road   → a (   ) road

4. a (silver / big) metal spoon   → a (   ) spoon

5. a (American / long / boring) movie → a (   ) movie

Exercise 2 Circle the correct form.

1. Kevin looked (interesting / interested) in what the commentator had said.

2. I know this is (embarrassing / embarrassed), but I fell asleep in the middle of the exam.

3. He is definitely one of the most (entertaining / entertained) guys I have ever met. He never stops talking about funny things.

4. The professor was (shocking / shocked) to know how many students in his lecture felt (boring / bored) with his talk.

Exercise 3 Complete the sentence by choosing the best word from the box.

disappointing / disappointed / amazing / amazed / boring / bored / terrifying / terrified

1. My roommate only talks about herself. I always feel (   ) listening to her.

2. The horror movie was (   ). I couldn't sleep at night.

3. She had never eaten such a wonderful dish. She looked (   ).

4. All the members of the team were crying because of the (   ) result.

Speaking Activity

TASK: The Little Red Riding Hood

Look at the pictures. With your partner take turns reading the story by filling in the blanks with adjectives.

Once upon a time, there lived a (   ) (   ) (   ) girl
called Little Red Riding Hood. She always wore a (   ) (   ) cape
that her grandma had made for her. One day, her mother said, "Your grandma is not well.
Please take this (   ) (   ) bread to her. Don't talk to strangers,
okay?"

Little Red Riding Hood set off to her grandmother's house on the other side of a forest. In the forest, she met a (   ) (   ) (   ) wolf.

The wolf said to her, "Look at these (   ) (   ) flowers? Why don't you pick some for your grandmother?" "What a wonderful idea," said Little Red Riding Hood and she began to pick them.

Meanwhile, the wolf ran to the grandmother's house and knocked on the
(   ) (   ) door. Knock, knock, knock. "Who's there?"
she asked. "Little Red Riding Hood," replied the wolf in his (   )
(   ) (   ) voice. Happy to find that her grandchild was
at the door, she said, "Come in, my darling." The wolf let himself in, and before the
(   ) (   ) grandmother could run away, the hungry wolf ate her!
Still hungry, he decided to wait for Little Red Riding Hood so that he could eat her too.

When Little Red Riding Hood got to her grandmother's house, she was a little confused.
"Grandma, what happened to you? Why have you got those (   )
(   ) ears?" "To hear you better," the wolf said. "Why have you got
those (   ) (   ) eyes?" she then asked. "To see you
better," he replied. "And why have you got those (   ) (   )
(   ) teeth?" she asked. "To eat you!" said the wolf and ate her in one gulp.

Come up with the ending for this story

_____

_____

_____

Listen to the story. Did you have the same adjectives? What did you think of the story?

CD (Disc 2): Track **11**

9

Scuffle at the Hotel

The target of this unit is to understand:

· *What / where / when*

Review Activity

Work in pairs. Arrange the adjectives to describe the pictures.

1. red / new / cool

2. brown / gigantic / strong-looking

3. unknown / large / horrible

4. old / tall / magnificent

Warm-Up

1. In what kind of situation do you feel nervous?
2. Do you think you can act calmly in an emergency?

Let's Watch!

Scene 9-1

Words and Phrases

CD (Disc 2): Track 12

tough: Mike is tough and has never lost a karate match.

frightened: The puppy is frightened of thunder.

Script of the Scene

CD (Disc 2): Track 13, 14 / DVD: Chapter 17 (20:23-21:20)

Vlad: She does not want to tell me. [1]( ) girl but stupid.

Sergey: Put the gun [2]( ). I am going to kill him [3]( ) you [4]( ).

Vlad: You are going to do that? [5]( )? No. You're [6]( ). No idea [7]( ) you're doing.

David: I do know [8]( ) I'm [9]( ).

Vlad: Look, we need the [10]( ) but I [11]( ) [12]( ) [13]( ) kill you. Sergey, tell him. We don't have to kill them, [14]( ) [15]( )? Just [16]( ) me the documents you [17]( ). And there's no problem. Everyone happy. Yes?

Olive: David, don't give [18]( ) to [19]( ).

Scene 9-2

Words and Phrases

CD (Disc 2): Track 15

Let's get down to it.: We don't have much time. Let's get down to it.

an only child: Deja is an only child and has always wanted a little sister.

can't stand ...: Turn off the music! I can't stand it.

Script of the Scene

CD (Disc 2): Track 16, 17 / DVD: Chapter 18 (21:21-22:10)

David: No, you're [20]( ).

Vlad: I am. All right, let's [21]( ) [22]( ) to it.

Sergey: What are you doing, Vlad?

Vlad: [23]( ) your father told me to do. David, your [24]( ) [25]( ).

David: Okay then, [26]( ) the killing [27]( ). Why [28]( ) we start with this guy. I [29]( ) [30]( ) him.

Sergey: No, no, no. Don't do that, please.

Vlad: Stop. Don't shoot. Please. Can't do this to your [31]( ), Sergey. You're his [32]( ) [33]( ).

Exercise 1 What did Gennady tell Vlad to do?

Exercise 2 True (T) or false (F)?

1. (　　) Sergey does not have any brothers and sisters.
2. (　　) David believes he and Olive can be saved if they give Vlad the document.
3. (　　) Olive refuses to give up the document.
4. (　　) Sergey lets Vlad kill David and Olive

Exercise 3 Answer the following questions.

1. What does Vlad want back from David and Olive?
   (　　　　　　　　　　　　　　　　　　　　　　　　　　　　　　　　　)
2. Why couldn't Vlad bring himself to shoot Olive and David?
   (　　　　　　　　　　　　　　　　　　　　　　　　　　　　　　　　　)
3. Why is Sergey's safety so important for Vlad?
   (　　　　　　　　　　　　　　　　　　　　　　　　　　　　　　　　　)
4. What does Vlad say will happen to David and Olive if they give him what he wants?
   (　　　　　　　　　　　　　　　　　　　　　　　　　　　　　　　　　)

Exercise 4 Discuss the following topics with your partners.

1. Do you have any siblings? Have you ever wanted brothers or sisters, or to be an only child?

2. What is something that would make you panic if it was stolen?

What / where / when

➜ **Used when we do not mention the noun that we are describing.**

This is just what we were looking for.

= This is just the thing (which / that) we were looking for

What happened yesterday was not my fault.

= The thing which/that happened yesterday was not my fault.

This is where the judge sits.

= This is the place (where / that) the judge sits.

She didn't tell us where she came from.

= She didn't tell us the place (where / that) she came from.

He is looking forward to when he'll be released from prison.

= He is looking forward to the day (when / that) he'll be released from prison.

The secret of success lies in when you start to work on it.

= The secret of success lies in the time (when / that) you start to work on it.

Exercise 1 **Correct a mistake in the sentence.**

1. I'm looking forward to what I graduate from university.

   → ( ).

2. I will never ever forgive when he did to me on that day.

   → ( ).

3. That was not when she lives. You went to the wrong house.

   → ( ).

Exercise 2 Reorder the words to make a sentence. The first word is not capitalized.

1. Long Field Theater is (him / I / supposed / meet / to / am / where). Not Long Field Museum.

    → Long Field Theater is (   ).

2. The first of April is (are / lies / people / tell / to / when / allowed).

    → The first of April is (   ).

3. If you want to work with us, tell me (company / you / for / do / can / our / what).

    → If you want to work with us,

    tell me (   ).

Exercise 3 Complete the sentence using the words in parentheses.

e.g., *Medicine* is _____ (*what / fever*)

    Medicine is ***what you take when you have a fever***.

1. School is _____ . (*where / subjects*)

2. A telephone is _____ . (*what / phone calls*)

3. Halloween is _____ . (*when / costume*)

Speaking Activity

TASK: What's the word?

Work in pairs. Person A, look at the four words on page 88. Person B, look at the words on page 101. Take turns describing the words. Continue describing until your partner gets it right.

e.g., *If you have the word "laptop," you can say:*

    It's what I use to do my homework.
    It's what I use to take online lessons.
    It's what I use to look for information on the internet.
    It's what I use to send e-mails.

 CD (Disc 2): Track 18

Listen and fill in the blanks.

Jimin: I'll be A, so can you be B?

Daiki: Okay. Then you can describe first. I'll guess the answer.

Jimin:: So, this is ₁ _____ to hang out ₂ _____ .

Daiki: You're gonna have to give me more than that.

Jimin:: I know I know. I just got started. This is ₃ _____ my friend and I

₄ _____ .

Daiki: Oh I think I know. But ₅ _____ , can you give me one more hint?

Jimin:: This is where ₆ _____ .

Daiki: It's ₇ _____ .

Jimin:: Correct!

Daiki: I ₈ _____ . Okay, my turn now.

Jimin:: I hope it's not too difficult.

Daiki: This is ₉ _____ my family and relatives

₁₀ _____ .

Jimin:: Is it ₁₁ _____ ?

Daiki: I'll give you another hint. It's ₁₂ _____ from my grandparents.

Jimin:: Ah! It's ₁₃ _____ !

Daiki: Yup! Good job!

[Unit **10**]

Taking Hostages

The target of this unit is to understand:

· Direct speech and reported speech
· Reported speech – time shift / pronoun change / questions

Review Activity

Look at the pictures and describe them by using *what*, *where*, or *when*.

1.

Chopsticks are ...

2.

The White House is ...

3.

December 25th is ...

Warm-Up

1. Have you ever tried to stop anyone from doing something bad or dangerous?
2. Have you ever changed your mind about something because it was dangerous or not a good idea?

 Let's Watch!

Scene 10-1

 **Words and Phrases** 🔊 CD (Disc 2) : Track 19

take ... for a ride: Mitchell took her for a ride in the riverside.

be after ...: The police were after the thief.

 **Script of the Scene** 🔊 CD (Disc 2) : Track 20, 21 / DVD: Chapter 19 (22:11-23:21)

Olive: We're [1]( ) your friend for a [2]( ). So, I don't want to see you [3]( ) us.

Vlad: You will. I'll [4]( ) [5]( ) you in no time.

Olive: Go.

......

Sergey: No, no. Please.

Scene 10-2

 **Words and Phrases** 🔊 CD (Disc 2) : Track 22

change one's mind: Chloe was going to the US to study, but she changed her mind when she found out about the tuition.

be about to ...: I was just about to leave when you called.

mobile phone: We can communicate with each other thanks to mobile phones.

track: How do police dogs track a scent?

retrieve: Our agent retrieved the bomb from the terrorist group.

apparently: Apparently, he was lying.

 **Script of the Scene** 🔊 CD (Disc 2) : Track 23, 24 / DVD: Chapter 20 (23:22-24:32)

David: What is that?

Olive: It's the door being [6]( ) [7]( ).

Sergey: He [8]( ) he'd be after you [9]( ) [10]( ) [11]( ). But I can still [12]( ) his [13]( ) if you just let me ... This doesn't have to [14]( ) [15]( ) people dying.

Olive: David. You're [16]( ) [17]( ) go for a ride.

Sergey: Please, no. I'll [18]( ) you how we found you.

Olive: How?

Sergey: The guy whose documents you stole gave him a [19]( ) [20]( ) that we can [21]( ). He [22]( ) my father to find you, [23]( ) the stuff, and apparently, also to kill you.

Sergey: Let's go, now.

Comprehension Check

Exercise 1 Why is Vlad on the ground?

Exercise 2 True (T) or false (F)?

1. (   ) Sergey wanted to change Vlad's mind.
2. (   ) Olive accepted Sergey's suggestion.
3. (   ) Gennady was asked to kill Olive and David.
4. (   ) Olive was given a mobile phone from the person whose documents were stolen.

Exercise 3 Answer the following questions.

1. What did Olive think caused the loud sound?
   (   )
2. Why did David throw away his mobile phone?
   (   )
3. How did Sergey and Vlad find Olive and David?
   (   )
4. Why did Sergey think he should change Vlad's mind?
   (   )

Exercise 4 Discuss the following topics with your partners.

1. What are some ways GPS can be useful?
2. What other apps on your mobile phone do you find useful?

Grammar

Direct speech and reported speech

➜ Direct speech: the words that people say

> I passed the examination.

> Congratulations!

➜ Reported speech: description of what someone said at an earlier point in time

> He said that he had passed the examination.

> He did it!

Reported speech – time shift

➜ **The tense of what was actually said in the direct speech changes in the reported speech (with the exception of the past perfect).**

Mary said, "I am busy now." (present simple)	She said she was busy. (past simple)
She said, "I am cooking dinner." (present continuous)	She said she was cooking dinner. (past continuous)
They said, "We have known each other for 5 years." (present perfect)	They said they had known each other for 5 years. (past perfect)
She said, "I have been working in the garden." (present perfect continuous)	She said she had been working in the garden. (past perfect continuous)
They said, "We didn't miss the bus." (past simple)	They said they hadn't missed the bus. (past perfect)
He said, "I was repairing my car the whole afternoon." (past continuous)	He said he had been repairing his car the whole afternoon. (past perfect continuous)
I said, "I had visited that place many times before 2012." (past perfect)	I said I had visited that place many times before 2012. (past perfect) (exception!)
He said, "I will come back soon." (future simple)	He said he would come back soon. (would)
I said, "I will not visit her again." (future simple)	I said I wouldn't visit her again. (would)

Notes

If the situation is still the same or a fact, it is not necessary to change the tense.

Mr. Tanaka said, "I don't like working for my boss."

Mr. Tanaka said that he doesn't like working for his boss.

My science teacher said, "Water boils at 100°C."

My science teacher said that water boils at 100°C.

Reported speech – pronoun change

Tom said, "I am enjoying your party."	Tom said he was enjoying my party.
My parents said, "We had a lovely weekend."	My parents said they had had a lovely weekend.
You said, "I will take care of your garden while you are away."	You said you would take care of my garden while I was away.

Reported speech – questions

Yes/No questions	(she) asked *if/whether* ...
He asked, "Are you hungry?"	He asked if I was hungry.
She asked me, "Were you satisfied with the result?"	She asked me whether I had been satisfied with the result.
*wh-*questions	(she) asked *when/where/who/how/why* ...
A friend asked me, "Where were you?"	A friend asked me where I had been.
She asked, "When are you going to bake the cake?"	She asked when we were going to bake the cake.

Notes

No inversion in reported speech for questions

O My teacher asked if I did my homework.

✕ My teacher asked if did I do my homework.

O I asked my friend what she ate for lunch.

✕ I asked my friend what did she eat for lunch.

Exercise 1 Read the dialogue and complete the reported speech.

1. Jade: When are you going to come back to Japan?
    You: I will be coming back in June.
    → You said that (   ) in June.

2. You: How many brothers do you have?
    Kate: Four.
    → Kate told you that (   ).

3. Kenji: What is the name of the restaurant we visited?
    His wife: I don't remember.
    → Kenji's wife said that (   ).

4. Pamela: How are you enjoying your new life in London?
    Dan: It's not as bad as I thought.
    → Dan told Pamela that his new life in London (   ).

Exercise 2 Change the direct speech into reported speech.

1. My brother said to me, "Do you happen to know her name?"
    → He asked (   ).

2. A man at customs said to us, "What is the purpose of your trip?"
    → He asked us (   ).

3. My mother said, "I'll cook curry and rice for dinner tonight."
    → She said that (   ).

4. A man in the street came over to me and said, "Where is the police station?"
    → A man in the street came over to me
      and asked (   ).

Exercise 3 Change all of what Mary said into reported speech.

e.g., "*What is your name?*"
    (*Mary asked me what my name is/was.*)

Mary

1. "What sports did you play when you were in high school?"
    (   )

2. "When will you graduate from university?"
    (   )

3. "Do you want to go to the movie with me next Saturday?"
    (   )

Speaking Activity

TASK: Talk about the happiest day of your life.

Step 1: Listen to Keita talk about the happiest day of his life. Take notes as you listen.

CD (Disc 2): Track 25

When was it?

_____

Who was/were there?

_____

What happened?

_____

Step 2: Check your answers with a partner. Use reported speech.

Keita said that his happiest day of his life was ...

Step 3: With a partner, take turns talking about the happiest day of your life. Take notes as you listen to your partner's story.

When was it?

_____

Who was/were there?

_____

What happened?

_____

Step 4: Find another pair and make a group. Take turns reporting the happiest day of the person you interviewed.

Listen and fill in the blanks.

Jimin: So tell me, Daiki, what was the happiest day of your life?

Daiki: I have to say, the happiest day of my life was ₁ _____

when I was ₂ _____ . I always ₃ _____

and ₄ _____ my parents for years to give me a dog. My

parents kept saying "no" because they were worried I would not be able to

₅ _____ it. But, finally, when I was six, they surprised me

with ₆ _____ . My parents and I ₇ _____

the Christmas tree to open presents. My dad went to their bedroom to get

another box and handed it to me. I ₈ _____ something

₉ _____ inside... And then when I ₁₀ _____ ,

there it was! The cutest puppy! ₁₁ _____ ! We are best friends

today and his name is Pochi.

······

Jimin: Hi everyone.

Bruno: Hi.

Tomoki: Hi.

Jimin: Let me tell you about Daiki's happiest day. It's really ₁₂ _____ .

He ₁₃ _____ his happiest day was Christmas Day when he

was six years old. He ₁₄ _____ to have a dog. His parents

₁₅ _____ to give him one because ₁₆ _____

that he would not have been able to care of a dog...

Argument in the Park

The target of this unit is to understand:
- *Because* vs. *because of*
- *This/that is becouse ...* vs. *This/that is why ...*
- *Feel like ...ing*

Review Activity

Work in pairs. Tell your partner what these people say.

1.

> I went to a botanical garden.
> I major in plant biology, so it was very interesting. Now, I can write my report on tropical flowers.

Cathy said ...

2.

> I came to Japan in 2020 to attend a university. I'm interested in architecture. I will visit Kyoto in March to visit old temples and shrines.

Mike said ...

Warm-Up

Talk with your partners.

1. Do you know what "blackmail" means?
2. Give an example of a blackmail.

Scene 11

 Words and Phrases

CD (Disc 2): Track 27

blackmail: She used the information to blackmail her boss.

care for: Paul and Camila broke up, but they still care for each other.

obvious: Why didn't you notice the obvious mistakes?

thug: The police officer shot at the thug.

matter: It doesn't matter to me whether he is correct or not.

presence: He didn't notice the presence of the cat.

distract: Please don't distract me. I need to concentrate!

vulnerable: Children are vulnerable and need protection.

include: The price includes the tax.

be on the point of ...ing: The company's finance is on the point of collapsing.

previous: Mark liked his previous job more.

leave ... alone: Please, just leave me alone. I don't want to talk to anyone.

the press: Unfortunately, the freedom of the press is sometimes restricted.

whatever: Whatever you may say, he won't forgive you for the mistake.

Give ... a second chance: I broke my friend's promise, but she gave me a second chance.

Script of the Scene

CD (Disc 2): Track 28, 29 / DVD: Chapter 21 (24:33-26:25)

Olive: So when were you gonna tell me you're working for Murray?

David: I'm not working for Murray. Okay, maybe I am ¹( )
²( ) Murray, but he ³( ) me into this. I was
⁴( ) ⁵( ) tell you but the Russian guys came and I
just ...

Olive: Blackmailed you? Is this why you wanted to find me?

David: No. I wanted to find you ⁶( ) I care for you. Why is it
⁷( ) to a Russian thug, but not to you?

......

Olive: I'm to deliver the documents to my ⁸( ) this evening. For
the time ⁹( ), this is all that ¹⁰( ). And you ...
I thought your ¹¹( ) would make it easier for me, but no.
You're ¹²( ) me, and making me vulnerable. I can't be
¹³( ) ¹⁴( ). This ¹⁵( ) has to take place
¹⁶( ).

David: Does it? ¹⁷( ) ¹⁸( ) the money you'll get?

Olive: No. You're not [19](   ) [20](   ) person being blackmailed here. I also need to [21](   ) the people I [22](   ) [23](   ). And that includes you.

David: You know, I was [24](   ) the [25](   ) of giving up on my previous life. But too many people can get hurt [26](   ) [27](   ) what we're doing. I'll tell Murray to [28](   ) you [29](   ). If not, I'll go to the [30](   ) with this thing. [31](   ) it is. You probably hate me right now, but if one day you [32](   ) [33](   ) giving us a [34](   ) [35](   ) ...

Comprehension Check

Exercise 1 Why is Olive angry at David? What excuse did David give?

Exercise 2 True (T) or false (F)?

1. (   ) Robert Murray blackmailed David.
2. (   ) Olive wants the transaction to be finished by the end of the day.
3. (   ) Both Olive and David were blackmailed.
4. (   ) David thinks that his decisions won't affect others.

Exercise 3 Answer the following questions.

1. Why did David want to find Olive?
   (   )

2. Who does Olive want to protect?
   (   )

3. What will David do if Murray does not leave Olive alone?
   (   )

4. What did David do to Olive at the end of the scene?
   (   )

Exercise 4 Discuss the following topics with your partners.

Do you wish you could have a second chance to do something again? What is it?

Because vs. *because of*

➜ Used to give reasons
because + sentence
My friend and I went to Ueno Zoo because we wanted to see some meerkats.
My family didn't travel this summer because the flight tickets were too expensive.
Did you fail the test because you didn't study?
because of + noun
My teacher didn't come to class today because of the flu.
Mr. Chen looked annoyed because of the parking ticket he received.
Were you late for class because of the train delay?

This/that is because ... vs. *this/that is why* ...

This/that is because ...
➜ Used to explain the reason or the cause of the result.
Result sentence. *This is because* ... (reason)
I had to turn back home. This is because I realized I had left my wallet.
We couldn't find Building 1. This was because we were at the wrong campus.
This/that is why ...
➜ Used to explain the result.
Reason sentence. *This is why* ... (result)
I realized I had left my wallet. This is why I had to turn back home.
We were at the wrong campus. That is why we couldn't find Building 1.

Feel like ...ing

→ **It is used to express what somebody wants.**

I feel like eating a cheeseburger. (= I want to eat a cheeseburger.)

He feels like being alone tonight. (=He wants to be alone tonight)

My friends and I don't feel like going clubbing this weekend. (= We don't want to go clubbing this weekend.)

Do you feel like eating out tonight? (= Do you want to eat out tonight?)

  –No, I'm too tired to go out. Let's just order some takeout.

Exercise 1 Fill in the blanks with either *because* or *because of* to complete the sentence.

1. The new product didn't sell well (   ) its poor quality.

2. I think she passed the test (   ) she worked so hard the night before.

3. He said he couldn't continue his work anymore (   ) his old age.

4. I need to call the manager (   ) I need more information.

Exercise 2 Fill in the blanks with *why* or *because* to complete the sentence.

1. Kevin and I had a big fight that night. That is (   ) we no longer talk to each other.

2. My computer suddenly broke down the other day. That's (   ) I need to buy a new one.

3. We have to get off this bus at the next stop. This is (   ) we are on the wrong bus.

4. My parents gave me a bike as a present. This is (   ) I passed the university exam.

Exercise 3 Rewrite the following sentences using *feel like*.

1. I would like to go to the lake on the weekend.

    → _____

2. My brother doesn't want to go to bed when it is too hot.

    → _____

3. We didn't want to talk about food then because we'd just eaten a lot.

    → _____

86

Speaking Activity

TASK: Board game

Make a small group. Take turns rolling a dice and making sentences with *This is because* ..., *This is why* ..., or *feel like*. You must complete the sentence in 10 seconds. If you cannot, you must stay on the same place and try again in your next turn.

Listen and fill in the blanks.

Jimin: Yay! Another board game!

Daiki: Okay. Let's ₁_____ to decide who goes first. Whoever has the highest number will start.

Bruno: ₂_____.

Daiki: Okay. I got a six. So I'll begin. I'll roll the dice again. It's a three.

Jimin: You have 10 seconds, Daiki.

Daiki: Whenever I have to study for an exam, I feel like … I feel like …

Bruno: Five seconds, Daiki.

Daiki: Ah! I feel like ₃_____.

Jimin: I ₄_____ how you feel. Me too. You just want to do ₅_____ study for the test, right?

Daiki: ₆_____! Bruno, it's your turn.

Bruno: All right. Let me roll the dice … Four! Oh no I have to skip a turn …

Speaking activity Unit 9
Person A's list: a frying pan, a compass, the library, Christmas

Vlad's Advice

The target of this unit is to understand:

· Passive voice: past simple/past perfect/future simple
· Passive voice: modal verbs

Review Activity

Take turns making sentences using *This is why ...*, *This is because,* and *feel like ...ing*.

1. I was late for the class today. This is because ...
2. We have to study English very hard. This is because ...
3. It's too hot. I can't stand it. I feel like ...
4. This music is amazing. I feel like ...
5. I won the lottery. This is why ...
6. This app is very useful. This is why ...

Warm-Up

1. Would you like to have the same profession as someone in your family? Why or why not?
2. What is important for you when looking for a job: Salary, working hours, contribution to society?

 Words and Phrases

(( )) CD (Disc 2) : Track 31

botch up: The new worker botched the project up.

trick: The car dealer tricked her into buying the used BMW.

obligation: Submitting a business report everyday is an obligation in this company.

brain: Studies of brains have rapidly developed lately.

imagine: I can't imagine that it'll rain tomorrow.

send: I'll be sending you a message on Messenger.

cool down: Let's have a break and cool down.

pretend: My daughter pretended to be sick so she could skip school.

turn ... into: The windmill turns wind into energy.

Script of the Scene

(( )) CD (Disc 2) : Track 32, 33 / DVD: Chapter 22 (26:26–28:49)

Vlad: You must tell him we ... er ...

Sergey: [1](   ) [2](   ) the killing?

Vlad: Botched up the killing.

Sergey: I don't give a shit. I've been [3](   ) [4](   ) him ... again. But he's always been like that. He says [5](   ) [6](   ), means [7](   ) [8](   ), but in the end ... it's all about [9](   ).

Vlad: But he is [10](   ) he is. Not much can [11](   ) [12](   ) to make him different. You need to understand his ... er ... [13](   ).

Sergey: Yeah? [14](   ) your family [15](   ) [16](   ) your obligations?

Vlad: No, they weren't. No. My [17](   ) was like you. Good student, strong brain. [18](   ) man like me, but didn't like [19](   ). He had a [20](   ) [21](   ), like you. Wanted to be a [22](   ). Can you imagine? My son ... a doctor? And my wife ... well ... She was ...

Sergey: They [23](   ) [24](   ), weren't they?

Vlad: Half a year ago. I found [25](   ) [26](   ) the men who came to my house [27](   ) [28](   ). Did bad things to them. Took my time. But too many questions [29](   ) [30](   ). So my bosses sent me to [31](   ) [32](   ). Cool down here.

Sergey: What am I [33](   ) to do now? Go back home? [34](   ) my dad didn't try to [35](   ) me [36](   ) a killer?

Scene 12-2

Words and Phrases

🔊 CD (Disc 2) : Track 34

lifestyle: Logan envies Lucas for his rich lifestyle.

heaps of: This new AI solves heaps of problems in a minute.

Script of the Scene

🔊 CD (Disc 2) : Track 35, 36 / DVD: Chapter 23 (28:50-29:22)

Vlad: Yes, go back to ³⁷(   ) ³⁸(   ). He's getting
³⁹(   ) and he will need you to ⁴⁰(   )
⁴¹(   ) his business. You'll get used to this ⁴²(   ) ...
girls, ⁴³(   ) ⁴⁴(   ) money. People pissing their pants
when they see you.

Sergey: Thank you, Vlad, but ⁴⁵(   ) ⁴⁶(   ) ⁴⁷(   ).

Comprehension Check

Exercise 1 Who called Sergey? Why didn't Sergey answer the phone?

Exercise 2 True (T) or false (F)?

1. (   ) Vlad's son wanted to be a doctor.
2. (   ) Vlad found the men who murdered his family.
3. (   ) Vlad was sent to the US.
4. (   ) Sergey agrees to take over his father's business.

Exercise 3 Answer the following questions.

1. Why is Sergey angry at his father?
   (   )
2. What was Vlad's son like?
   (   )
3. Why did Gennady send Vlad to the UK?
   (   )
4. What did Vlad tell Sergey are the advantages of doing the same job as his father's?
   (   )

Exercise 4 Discuss the following topics with your partners.

1. What are three adjectives to describe your personality?
2. Whose personality do you take after in your family?

Passive voice: past simple / past perfect / future simple

Passive voice = *be* + past participle
was/were + past participle He was given the telephone number for Olive Green, a professional art thief. Was *Romeo and Juliet* written by Shakespeare?
had been + Past Participle When Robert opened the safety deposit box, the documents had already been stolen. The castle had not been restored until 1770.
will be + Past Participle The transaction between Olive and her boss will be finalized in a few hours. Will the museum be closed during the Christmas holiday?

Passive voice: modal verbs

---

should / may / might / can / could / must (*not*) + *be* + past participle

You may (not) be asked to answer all the questions in detail.

You might (not) be given additional information.

Can this error be fixed immediately?

The door could (not) be painted a different color immediately.

Cars must (not) be parked here.

Should the report be prepared by our department?

Exercise 1 Use the provided verb to complete the sentence. The tense is given in [ ].

e.g., *paint [past simple]*

    *a) I (**painted**) a beautiful picture in my art class.*

    *b) Sunflowers (**was painted**) by Vincent van Gogh.*

1. invent [past simple]

    a) My father (   ) a machine to automatically water

        plants in the garden some years ago.

    b) The television (   ) by Philo Farnsworth.

2. use [past perfect]

    a) For many centuries, this drug (   ) to treat medical

        conditions.

    b) People (   ) Latin for many years.

3. delay [future simple]

    a) The train (   ) because of the heavy rain.

    b) The sudden typhoon (   ) their flight to Hawaii.

Exercise 2 Complete the sentences using the verbs in the box in the passive. You cannot use the same word twice.

| steal | speak | do | bite | repair |

1. The construction has not started yet. I think the road should (   ) immediately.

2. Were you (   ) by the neighbor's dog? He's so violent, isn't he?

3. When he opened the safe, he found that the document had (   ).

4. Fewer and fewer languages will (   ) in the years to come.

5. Something must (   ) to prevent the rise of the global temperature.

Exercise 3 Reorder the words to make a sentence. The first word is not capitalized.

1. (arrested / by / the thief / the police officer / was) yesterday.
   → _____

2. (by / be / an adult / must / under / accompanied / children / the age of twelve).
   → _____

3. (been / the emergency brake / stop / had / applied / to) the train?
   → _____ the train?

4. (discovered / will / be / until / the criminal / not / the truth) is arrested.
   → _____ is arrested.

TASK: Name a thing

Make a group of three people. Read the instructions aloud. The first person to answer gets two points, the second person one point, and the last person to give a response, or the person who cannot give a response gets zero points. You also cannot get a point if you cannot give a response in the passive voice. Before you start, make 3 of your own questions (for #7-9) to ask your peers.

		Player 1	Player 2	Player 3
e.g.,	*Name a popular dish that is eaten in Italy.*	0	2	1
1	Name something that had been invented before you were born.			
2	Name a sport that cannot be played alone.			
3	Name a singer who was born in Japan.			
4	Name a film that was shown this year.			
5	Name an event that will be held in the next five years.			
6	Name a song that was popular last year.			
7				
8				
9				

Listen and fill in the blanks.

Jimin: This game looks difficult! Let's start! It says, "Name a popular dish that is eaten in Italy."

Daiki: I got it! ₁ _____ is a dish that ₂ _____ in Italy.

Bruno: Okay, that's two points for Daiki. Man, you were fast.

Jimin: I got one too. It's ₃ _____.

Daiki: Good answer Jimin, but ₄ _____ you didn't make a sentence in the passive voice.

Jimin: Oh no! I guess I don't get a point then.

Bruno: Wait, does that mean I ₅ _____?

Daiki: Yeah, I ₆ _____.

Bruno: Well, I'll take my ₇ _____ to come up with one then.

Jimin: Hahaha. C'mon Bruno, we have a long list to go through.

Bruno: Okay then. ₈ _____ is ₉ _____ many people in Italy.

Daiki: Fine, that's a point for you.

97

[Review 2]

1 **Read the situation and complete the sentence using the past perfect tense.**

e.g., *You met your ex-boyfriend for the first time in 10 years yesterday.*
  → *(I / not / see him for a long time)* **I hadn't seen him for a long time**.

1. My sister was watching a movie. You didn't know it.
   → (I / not / see / it / before).

   _____

2. The girl sitting next to me on the roller coaster was nervous. It was her first time riding it.
   → (She / not / ride / before).

   _____

3. You went to visit your grandparents' recently after five years. it wasn't the same as before.
   → (It / change / a lot)

   _____

4. I offered the guests something to eat, but they weren't hungry.
   → (They / just / had / a big meal)

   _____

2 **Choose the past simple or the past perfect tense to complete the sentence.**

1. We had already finished dinner when my sister _____ (come) home.

2. I opened my backpack to find that I _____ (forgot) my wallet. When we _____ (arrive) at the station, the train had already left.

3. We got home to find that someone _____ (break) into the house.

4. After arriving home, I realized I _____ (not / buy) any food for dinner.

98

3 Put the adjectives in the correct order.

1. a (French / pretty) doll   → a (   ) doll

2. a(n) (old / steel) knife   → a(n) (   ) knife

3. a (red / small) spider   → a (   ) spider

4. a (green / large) rug   → a (   ) rug

5. (ancient / silk) clothes   → (   ) clothes

4 Circle the correct form.

1. The child seems (frightening / frightened) by the lion in the zoo.

2. My colleague, Anna, is an (annoying / annoyed) person because she is always talking to me even when I am very busy.

3. (Pleasing / Pleased) dogs shake their tails when they receive treats.

4. We found a very (interesting / interested) insect in our yard.

5. The news that a capybara killed a Japanese monkey is very (surprising / surprised).

5 Correct a mistake in the sentence.

1. A calculator is that you use to solve math problems.

    → (   )

2. Elementary schools are when children study.

    → (   )

3. December 31st is what a year ends.

    → (   )

6 Complete the sentence using the words in parentheses.

e.g., *Medicine is _____ (what / fever)*

     Medicine is **what you take when you have a fever.**

1. A hotel is _____ (where / travelers)

2. Wifi is _____ (what / the Internet)

3. 1945 is _____ (when / WWII)

7 **Read the dialogue and complete the reported speech.**

1. Mike: Where are you planning to go during the summer holidays?
   Toru: I'm going to my uncle's in Karuizawa.
   → Toru said that (   ).

2. Olive: Do you love me or not?
   David: Of course, I do.
   → Olive asked David (   ).

3. Sergey: Do I need to use the gun?
   Vlad: You have to.
   → Vlad said that (   ).

4. Sofia: How old were you when you graduated from college?
   Ivan: 22.
   → Sofia asked Ivan (   ).

8 **Olive is talking to David. Change all of what Olive said into reported speech.**

1. "Do you want to run away with me?"
   (   )

2. "What is the best way to escape this situation?"
   (   )

3. "I had done many bad things before."
   (   )

4. "I'm not going to give up, whatever happens."
   (   )

9 **Fill in the blanks with *why* or *because* to complete the sentence.**

1. I was extremely angry. This is (   ) I had been shouting at him.

2. He needed to work really hard that night. This is (   ) the deadline for his assignment was due the next day.

3. I've always wanted to meet you in person. This is (   ) I'm here today.

4. The police didn't arrive on time. This is (   ) there was a lot of traffic on the way.

10 Rewrite the following sentences using *feel like*.

1. My brother wants to go to a party tonight.

→ _____

2. Because I was tired, I didn't want to meet up with friends.

→ _____

3. Do you want to get some coffee?

→ _____

11 Reorder the words to make a sentence. The first word is not capitalized.

1. (our anniversary dinner / a famous chef / by / cooked / was)

→ _____

2. (babies / be / by / parents / should / small / watched) all day.

→ _____ all day

3. (announced / been / had / of the exam / the date)?

→ _____ ?

4. (be / by this week / fixed / not / the computer / will)

→ _____

12 Complete the sentences using the verbs in the box in the passive. You cannot use the same word twice.

take	do	move	hold	develop

1. The table in the living room must ( ) to the kitchen.

2. New interests can easily ( ) in the minds of young children.

3. Babies must ( ) care of with much affection from their parents.

4. A meeting should ( ) immediately. There's something we need to discuss.

Speaking activity Unit 9
Person B's list: a passport, scissors, a cafeteria, Obon

オリーブ・グリーン：
ミステリードラマで学ぶ実用英語（CEFR-B1）

検印
省略

©2023 年 1 月 31 日　第 1 版発行

編著者　　　　　　　　　浅利　庸子
　　　　　　　　　　　　菅野　　悟
　　　　　　　　　　　　久保　岳夫
　　　　　　　　　　　　佐藤　亮輔
　　　　　　　　　　　　SIMPSON William

発行者　　　　　　　　　小川　洋一郎
発行所　　　　　　　　株式会社 朝日出版社
　　　　　〒101-0065 東京都千代田区西神田 3-3-5
　　　　　　　　電話　東京　(03) 3239-0271
　　　　　　　　FAX　東京　(03) 3239-0479
　　　　　　E-mail　text-e@asahipress.com
　　　　　　　　振替口座　00140-2-46008
　　　　　　　　http://www.asahipress.com/
　　　　　組版／メディアアート　製版／図書印刷

ISBN 978-4-255-15699-6

9784255156996

1921082024007

ISBN978-4-255-15699-6

C1082 ¥2400E

円 (本体2400円+税10%)

客注